DID YOU KNOW THIS WAS IN THE BIBLE,
The Greatest Book Ever Written?

A Guidance Book For Living Your Life Today

CAROLE WILLIAMS

Bible verses are taken from the original King James

Version

DEDICATION

I want to give all the honor, praise and glory to my Lord and Savior, Jesus Christ for giving me the guidance to write this book.   I love him with all my heart and soul.

This book is dedicated to my daughter, our beautiful family, to my wonderful friends, pastor, to our readers, and especially to my Lord.

A very special thanks to my friend, Vicki Shankwitz for her help and inspiration. Vicki is an accomplished author in her own right, and her works can be found on the Internet.

As you read this book, please note that all the words JESUS SPOKE HIMSELF ARE WRITTEN IN RED.

IF THIS BOOK TOUCHES JUST <u>ONE LIFE</u>
AND THAT PERSON IS <u>SAVED</u>, THEN ALL
MY EFFORTS WILL NOT HAVE BEEN IN VAIN.
HOPEFULLY, MANY, MANY PEOPLE WILL READ
THIS BOOK AND BE SAVED.

THERE ARE SO MANY THINGS CONTAINED IN
THE BIBLE THAT APPLY TO OUR SOCIETY
TODAY.

IF YOU READ THIS BOOK FROM COVER TO COVER, YOU'LL DISCOVER SOME OF THOSE AMAZING THINGS THAT I'LL BET YOU DIDN'T KNOW WERE IN THE BIBLE!

<u>TAKEN FROM THE ORIGINAL KING JAMES VERSION.</u>

CONTENTS

AUTHOR'S THOUGHTS

First of all, I would like to say that this book is not written for Biblical Scholars or those trained in seminary. It is intended for those people who have not studied their Bible for a long time, for those who have never read the Bible, and for those who have never come to know our Lord and Savior, Jesus Christ.

I believe EVERY WORD in the Bible is TRUE, whether it be Old Testament or New Testament.

II Samuel 7:28: And now, O Lord God, thou art that God, and thy words be true, and thou hast promised this goodness unto thy servant.

Revelation 22:6: And he said unto me, These sayings are faithful and true: and the Lord God of the holy prophets sent his angel to show unto his servants the things which must shortly be done.

The Lord has been good to me as He allowed me to be raised in a Christian home. However, as I grew older, I realized that there were a lot of people who had never, ever been to a church or read the Holy Bible. Learning about God and his commandments is the beginning of wisdom.

Hebrews Chapter 13

Verse 15 says: By him therefore let us offer the sacrifice of praise to God continually, that is, the fruit of our lips giving thanks to his name.

Verse 16 says: But to do good and to communicate forget not: for with such sacrifices God is well pleased.

The Bible truly is the most amazing book ever written.

Psalm 24:1: The earth is the Lord's, and the fullness thereof; the world, and they that dwell therein.

Even though our Lord ascended to Heaven and left behind the cross, a crown of thorns, and an earthly garment, he is still always with us for comfort and strength.

JESUS ASCENDS INTO HEAVEN

<u>Luke 24:50:</u>   And he led them out as far as to Bethany, and he lifted up his hands, and blessed them.

<u>Luke 24:51:</u>   And it came to pass, while he blessed them, he was parted from them, and carried up into heaven.

"THINGS LEFT BEHIND"

Artist: Carole Williams
(c) 2016

These are four of my favorite Bible scriptures:

Psalm 24:1: The earth is the Lord's, and the fulness thereof; the world, and they that dwell therein.

Wow, what a powerful statement!

II Corinthians 1:3-5
Verse 3: Blessed be God, even the Father of our Lord Jesus Christ, the Father of mercies, and the God of all comfort.
Verse 4: Who comforteth us in all our tribulation, that we may be able to comfort them which are in any trouble, by the comfort wherewith we ourselves are comforted of God.
Verse 5: For as the sufferings of Christ abound in us, so our consolation also aboundeth by Christ.

The Bible contains SO MUCH knowledge and wisdom for us to apply to our daily lives.

I want to ask each person reading this book to not only read each verse printed here, but to read additional verses before and after each verse.

The Book of Proverbs provides good wisdom and offers to us guidelines as to how we should live our lives.

It had been quite a few years since I had studied my Bible in depth, and again, the amazing things I discovered were amazing!

Explore your Bible as I did for amazing miracles and the parables that Jesus taught.

As I began studying, I found things that I never knew were in the Bible! See the section on SUBJECTS, A-Z.

You may find duplication of some verses, but it is to emphasize the importance of particular subjects.

This book has three main purposes:

> To bring souls to Christ
>
> To encourage others to study the Bible and learn more about Jesus Christ and his wonderful teachings.
>
> To reconnect you to your Lord, so that you will have a daily PERSONAL RELATIONSHIP with Him.

As you begin to STUDY and PRAY, you will see your life change. You will see what the Lord wants all of us to do.

You will realize how much the Lord just wants us to keep his commandments and bring others to Him.

<u>Matthew 6:33</u>: But seek ye first the kingdom of God, and his righteousness; and all these things shall be added unto you.

<u>Luke 12:29-31</u>
<u>Verse 29</u>: And seek not ye what ye shall eat, or what ye shall drink, neither be ye of doubtful mind.
<u>Verse 30</u>: For all these things do the nations of the world seek after: and your Father knoweth that ye have need of these things.
<u>Verse 31</u>: But rather seek ye the kingdom of God; and all these things shall be added unto you.

Is he telling us that the worldly things don't matter, that we should love one another, help the poor, and spread his gospel to all the world?

We can't take any material things with us when we pass on, but we can be steadfast in telling others about the words of Jesus and his saving grace.

WHAT <u>WOULD</u> JESUS DO? Shouldn't this be our life's motto in deciding what is right or wrong?

I am including some of my personal Christian artwork and personal writings as my gift to you.

May each one of you reading this book make Jesus FIRST in your life. If you do this, you will see a remarkable difference in HIS time frame, and you will be amazed at the many, many blessings you will receive as you turn your life over to him.

God Bless you!

Carole Williams, Author
© 2016

THE TEN COMMANDMENTS

Deuteronomy 5:7-21

Verse 7: Thou shalt have none other gods before me.

Verse 8: Thou shalt not make thee any graven image, or any likeness of any thing that is in heaven above, or that is in the earth beneath, or that is in the waters beneath the earth.

Verse 9: Thou shalt not bow down thyself unto them, nor serve them: for I the Lord thy God am a jealous God, visiting the iniquity of the fathers upon the children unto the third and fourth generation of them that hate me.

Verse 11: Thou shalt not take the name of the Lord thy God in vain: for the Lord will not hold him guiltless that taketh his name in vain.

Verse 12: Keep the Sabbath day to sanctify it, as the Lord thy God hath commanded thee.

Verse 16: Honor thy father and thy mother, as the Lord thy God hath commanded thee; that thy days may be prolonged, and that it may go well with thee, in the land which the Lord thy God giveth thee.

<u>Verse 17</u>: Thou shalt not kill.

<u>Verse 18</u>: Neither shalt thou commit adultery.

<u>Verse 19</u>: Neither shalt thou steal.

<u>Verse 20</u>: Neither shalt thou bear false witness against thy neighbor.

<u>Verse 21</u>: Neither shalt thou desire thy neighbor's wife, neither shalt thou covet thy neighbor's house, his field, or his manservant, or his maidservant, his ox, or his ass, or any thing that is thy neighbor's.

SUMMARY OF THE LIFE OF JESUS

Jesus was born
Matthew Chapter 2, Verses 1-11

Jesus prophesied on the Mt. Of Olives
Matthew Chapter 24, Verses 3-35

Jesus performed miracles and healing
John Chapter 2, Verse 11
John Chapter 2, Verse 23
John Chapter 6, Verse 2
John Chapter 11, Verse 47
John Chapter 12:37

Jesus was tormented and ridiculed
Mark Chapter 15, Verses 17-37

Jesus was crucified
Matthew Chapter 27, Verse 45
Mark Chapter 15, Verse 25

Jesus was buried in the sepulchre
Matthew Chapter 27, Verses 57-60

God's Angel came and rolled away the stone
Matthew Chapter 28, Verses 2-8

Jesus rose on the third day

Matthew Chapter 27, Verses 63-66
Matthew Chapter 28, Verses 1-6
Romans Chapter 10, Verse 9
Luke Chapter 24, Verse 46

Jesus ascended to Heaven

Luke Chapter 24, Verses 46-51

BECOMING A CHRISTIAN IS EASY

Find a church. - Jesus often spoke of the churches:
Revelation 2:7
He that hath an ear, let him hear what the Spirit saith
unto the churches: To him that overcometh will I give
to eat of the tree of life, which is in the midst of the
paradise of God.
Revelation 22:16
I Jesus have sent mine angel to testify unto you these
things in the churches. I am the root and the
offspring of David, and the bright and morning star.

I Corinthians 7:17
But as God hath distributed to every man, as the Lord
hath called every one, so let him walk. And so ordain
I in all churches.
I Corinthians 14:33
For God is not the author of confusion, but of peace,
as in all churches of the saints.

Repent of your sins. Confess with your mouth that
you believe Jesus is Lord, believe he was crucified
and resurrected the third day.
Romans 10:9-10
Verse 9: That if thou shalt confess with thy mouth the
Lord Jesus, and shalt believe in thine heart that God
hath raised him from the dead, thou shalt be saved.

Verse 10: For with the heart man believeth unto righteousness; and with the mouth confession is made unto salvation.

Hebrews 10:16-17
Verse 16: This is the covenant that I will make with them after those days, saith the Lord, I will put my laws into their hearts, and in their minds will I write them.
Verse 17: And their sins and iniquities will I remember no more.

Mark 1:15
And saying, The time is fulfilled, and the kingdom of God is at hand; repent ye, and believe the gospel.

Be Baptized
Acts 19:4
Then said Paul, John verily baptized with the baptism of repentance, saying unto the people, that they should believe on him which should come after him, that is, on Christ Jesus.

Ephesians 4:5
One Lord, one faith, one baptism.

The Promise
Ephesians 1:20-23
Verse 20: Which he wrought in Christ, when he raised him from the dead, and set him at his own right hand in the heavenly places.

<u>Verse 21</u>: Far above all principality, and power, and might, and dominion, and every name that is named, not only in this world, but also <u>in that which is to come.</u>
<u>Verse 22:</u> And hath put all things under his feet, and gave him to be the head over all things to the church.
<u>Verse 23:</u> Which is his body, the fullness of him that filleth all in all.

<u>Study the Bible, and keep God's Commandments.</u>
Your days will be prolonged if you keep God's commandments. Enjoy the fellowship at your new church, there will always be supportive church members who have shared the same circumstances in life that you have.

<u>Deuteronomy 4:40</u>: Thou shalt keep therefore his statutes, and his commandments, which I command thee this day, that it may go well with thee, and with thy children after thee, and that thou mayest prolong thy days upon the earth, which the Lord thy God giveth thee, for ever.

Enjoy the fellowship at your new church, there will always be supportive church members who have shared the same circumstances in life that you have.

When you are baptized, <u>your sins will be forgiven.</u>
You will begin a new life in our Lord, Jesus Christ,
keeping his commandments, and enjoying a
wonderful new beginning. All of us will sin again
after baptism, but our sins can be forgiven.

<u>II Corinthians 5:17-18</u>
<u>Verse 17</u>: Therefore if any man be in Christ, he is a
new creature; old things are passed away; behold, all
things are become new.
<u>Verse 18</u>: And all things are of God, who hath
reconciled us to himself by Jesus Christ, and hath
given to us the ministry of reconciliation.

<u>John 3:3</u>: Jesus answered and said unto him, Verily,
verily, I say unto thee, Except a man be born again,
he cannot see the kingdom of God.
<u>John 3:5</u>: Jesus answered, Verily, verily, I say unto
thee, Except a man be born of water and of the Spirit,
he cannot enter into the kingdom of God.

<u>Psalm 145:19-20</u>
<u>Verse 19</u>: He will fulfill the desire of them that fear
him; he also will hear their cry, and will save them.
<u>Verse 20</u>: The Lord preserveth all them that love him;
but all the wicked will he destroy.

Hebrews 10:16-17

Verse 16: This is the covenant that I will make with them after those days, saith the Lord, I will put my laws into their hearts, and in their minds will I write them.

Verse 17: And their sins and iniquities will I remember no more.

Luke 15:7: I say unto you, that likewise joy shall be in heaven over one sinner that repenteth, more than over ninety and nine just persons, which need no repentance.

HOW TO BE SAVED AND FORGIVEN OF YOUR SINS

Romans 10:11-13
Verse 11: For the scripture saith, Whosoever believeth on him shall not be ashamed.
Verse 12: For there is no difference between the Jew and the Greek; for the same Lord over all is rich unto all that call upon him.
Verse 13: For whosoever shall call upon the name of the Lord shall be saved.

Romans 3:23: For all have sinned, and come short of the glory of God.

II Corinthians 5:17-18
Verse 17: Therefore if any man be in Christ, he is a new creature; old things are passed away; behold, all things are become new.
Verse 18: And all things are of God, who hath reconciled us to himself by Jesus Christ, and hath given to us the ministry of reconciliation.

Matthew 9:12-13
Verse 12: But when Jesus heard that, he said unto them, They that be whole need not a physician, but they that are sick.
Verse 13: But go ye and learn what that meaneth, I will have mercy, and not sacrifice; for I am not come to call the righteous, but sinners to repentance.

<u>Acts 3:19</u>: Repent ye therefore; and be converted, that your sins may be blotted out, when the times of refreshing shall come from the presence of the Lord.

<u>Luke 15:7</u>: I say unto you, that likewise joy shall be in heaven over one sinner that repenteth, more than over
ninety and nine just persons, which need no repentance.

<u>Luke 15:10</u>: Likewise, I say unto you, there is joy in the presence of the angels of God over one sinner that
 repenteth.

<u>Isaiah 53:6</u>: All we like sheep have gone astray; we have turned every one to his own way; and the Lord hath laid on him the iniquity of us all.

<u>John 3:16</u>: For God so loved the world, that he gave his only begotten Son, that whosoever believeth in him should not perish, but have everlasting life.
<u>John 3:17</u>: For God sent not his Son into the world to condemn the world; but that the world through him might be saved.

THE SECOND COMING OF JESUS CHRIST

The following is a summary of the SIGNS of Jesus' **_SECOND COMING_** to earth, found in Matthew Chapter 24, Verses 3 through 8, and found in Matthew Chapter 24, Verses 21-36:

- There will be anti-Christs.
- There will be wars and rumors of wars.
- Nations shall rise against nations, and kingdom against kingdom.
- There will be famines.
- There will be Pestilences.
- There will be earthquakes in diver's places.
- People shall be afflicted.
- People will be killed.
- People will be hated of all nations for the Lord's sake.
- Many will be offended.
- Many will betray one another.
- Many shall hate one another.
- Many false Prophets shall rise and deceive many.
- Because iniquity (sin) shall abound, the love of many shall wax cold.
- This gospel of the kingdom shall be preached in all the world for a witness unto all nations, and then shall the end come...

<u>Mark 13:30-33</u>

<u>Verse 30</u>: Verily I say unto you, that this generation shall not pass, till all these things be done.

<u>Verse 31</u>: Heaven and earth shall pass away, but my words shall not pass away.

<u>Verse 32</u>: But of that day and that hour knoweth no man, no, not the angels which are in heaven, neither the Son, but the Father.

<u>Verse 33</u>: Take ye heed, watch and pray, for ye know not when the time is.

DID YOU KNOW
THIS WAS IN THE BIBLE?

ACCOUNT

The Bible tells us that all of us shall give account of ourselves to God.

Romans 14:12-13

Verse 12: So then every one of us shall give account of himself to God.

Verse 13: Let us not therefore judge one another any more; but judge this rather, that no man put a stumblingblock or an occasion to fall in his brother's way.

ANATHEMA MARANTHA

Do you know what the phrase "Anathema Marantha" means?

I Corinthians 16:22: If any man love not the Lord Jesus Christ, let him be Anathema Maranatha.

ANGELS

Did you know that God's Angel rolled back the stone at the sepulchre that Jesus was buried in? And, the angel sat upon it?

Matthew 28:2: And, behold, there was a great earthquake; for the angel of the Lord descended from heaven, and came and rolled back the stone from the door, and sat upon it.

ANGELS-CHARGE OVER THEE

Did you know the Bible says the Lord shall give his angels charge over thee?

Psalm 91:9-11

Verse 9: Because thou hast made the Lord, which is my refuge, even the most High, thy habitation;

Verse 10: There shall no evil befall thee, neither shall any plague come nigh thy dwelling.

Verse 11: For he shall give his angels charge over thee, to keep thee in all thy ways.

ANGER OF JESUS

Did you know that Jesus got very angry because the temple was used as a house of merchandise?

John 2:13-16

Verse 13: And the Jews' Passover was at hand, and Jesus went up to Jerusalem.

Verse 14: And found in the temple those that sold oxen and sheep and doves, and the changers of money sitting.

Verse 15: And when he had made a scourge of small cords, he drove them all out of the temple, and the sheep, and the oxen, and poured out the changers' money, and overthrew the tables.

Verse 16: And said unto them that had sold doves, Take these things hence; make not my Father's house an house of merchandise.

ANSWERS

Did you know the Bible cautions us about the words we speak? A soft answer is commendable.

Proverbs 15:1-2

Verse 1: A soft answer turneth away wrath; but grievous words stir up anger.

Verse 2: The tongue of the wise useth knowledge aright; but the mouth of fools poureth out foolishness.

ANGRY MEN

The Bible cautions us to choose our friends carefully.

Proverbs 22:24-25

Verse 24: Make no friendship with an angry man; and with a furious man thou shalt not go.

Verse 25: Lest thou learn his ways, and get a snare to thy soul.

ASCENTION/DESCENTION

The Bible says Jesus came from Heaven and returned to Heaven.

John 16:28: I came forth from the Father, and am come into the world: again, I leave the world, and go to the Father.

ASHAMED OF JESUS

The Bible says we should NEVER be ashamed of Jesus.

Mark 8:38: Whosoever therefore shall be ashamed of me and of my words in this adulterous and sinful generation, of him also shall the Son of man be ashamed, when he cometh in glory of his Father with the holy angels.

APPEARANCE
In the Bible, it says we should not judge people by their appearance, but that we should respect them for their righteousness.

John 7:24: Judge not according to the appearance, but judge righteous judgment.

BAKED AND FRIED FOODS
The Bible actually mentions foods that are FRIED and BAKED.

I Chronicles 23:29: Both for the showbread, and for the fine flour for meat offering, and for the unleavened cakes, and for that which is baked in the pan, and for that which is fried, and for all manner of measure and size.

BARBER'S RAZOR AND A BEARD
Did you know that the Bible addresses a **barber's razor** and a **man's beard**?

Ezekiel 5:1: And THOU, son of man, take thee a sharp knife, take thee a barber's razor, and cause it to pass upon thine head and upon thy beard; then take thee balances to weigh, and divide the hair.

BEES
The Bible mentions bees chasing people.

Deuteronomy 1:44: And the Amorites, which dwelt

in that mountain, came out against you, and chased you, as bees do, and destroyed you in Seir, even unto Hormah.

BELCH OUT
Can you believe the Bible even mentions people "belching out with their mouths"?
Psalm 59:6-8
Verse 6: They return at evening; they make a noise like a dog, and go round about the city.
Verse 7: Behold, they belch out with their mouth; swords are in their lips; for who, say they, doth hear?
Verse 8: But thou, O Lord, shall laugh at them; thou shalt have all the heathen in derision.

BODY-NATURAL BODY AND SPIRITUAL BODY
Is the Bible telling us we have a natural, physical body here on earth, but when we die our spirits leave and go to Heaven?
I Corinthians 15:44: It is sown a natural body; it is raised a spiritual body. There is a natural body, and there is a spiritual body.

BONNETS-LINEN BONNETS UPON THEIR HEADS
A reference in the Bib mentions "linen bonnets" on their heads, way back in Jesus' time.
Ezekiel 44:18: They shall have linen bonnets upon their heads, and shall have linen breeches upon their loins; they shall not gird themselves with any thing that causeth sweat.

BOOK OF LIFE

The Bible tells us about God's "Book of Life" for those on earth who overcome sin.

Revelation 3:5: He that overcometh, the same shall be clothed in white raiment; and I will not blot out his name out of the book of life, but I will confess his name before my Father, and before his angels.

Revelation 20:15: And whosoever was not found written in the book of life was cast into the lake of fire.

BORROWERS

The Bible explains that the borrower is a servant to the lender; doesn't the same wisdom apply today?

Proverbs 22:7: The rich ruleth over the poor, and the borrower is servant to the lender.

BRAWLERS

In the Bible, it tells us NOT to be "brawlers", but to be gentle and show meekness unto all men.

Titus 3:2-4

Verse 2: To speak evil of no man, to be no brawlers, but gentle, showing all meekness unto all men.

Verse 3: For we ourselves also were sometimes foolish, disobedient, deceived, serving divers lusts and pleasures, living in malice and envy, hateful, and hating one another.

Verse 4: But after that the kindness and love of God our Saviour toward man appeared.

A BROTHER'S TRESPASS AND FORGIVENESS

We are admonished in the Bible to forgive our brother's trespass over and over again if he repents.

Luke 17:3-4

Verse 3: Take heed to yourselves; If thy brother trespass against thee, rebuke him; and if he repent, forgive him.

Verse 4: And if he trespass against thee seven times in a day, and seven times in a day turn again to thee, saying, I repent; thou shalt forgive him.

CALL UPON ME

Did you know the Bible talks about great and mighty things, which we knowest not?

Jeremiah 33:3: Call unto me, and I will answer thee, and show thee great and mighty things, which thou knowest not.

CAMEL AND A NEEDLE'S EYE

A discussion is made in the Bible about how hard it is for a rich man to enter into the Kingdom of God.

Luke 18:25-27

Verse 25: For it is easier for a camel to go through a needle's eye, than for a rich man to enter into the kingdom of God.

Verse 26: And they that heard it said, Who then can be saved?

Verse 27: And he said, The things which are impossible with men are possible with God.

CATERPILLARS

Did you know the Bible talks about worms and caterpillars and the insect chain?

Joel 1:4: That which the palmerworm hath left hath the locust eaten; and that which the locust hath left hath the cankerworm eaten; and that which the cankerworm hath left hath the caterpillar eaten.

CHANGED-WE SHALL ALL BE CHANGED

The Bible says that when Jesus comes again, we shall all be changed.

I Corinthians 15:51-52

Verse 51: Behold, I show you a mystery; We shall not all sleep, but we shall all be changed.

Verse 52: In a moment, in the twinkling of an eye, at the last trump; for the trumpet shall sound, and the dead shall be raised incorruptible, and we shall be changed.

CHARITY-FAITH, HOPE AND CHARITY

In the Bible, it tells us that the GREATEST of these three is CHARITY.

I Corinthians 13:13: And now abideth faith, hope, charity, these three; but the greatest of these is charity.

CHEERFUL GIVER

Did you know that God expects us to be CHEERFUL givers?

II Corinthians 9:7: Every man according as he

purposeth in his heart, so let him give; not grudgingly, or of necessity; for God loveth a cheerful giver.

CHILD/CHILDISH THINGS
This verse tells us that we should put away childish things.
I Corinthians 13:11: When I was a child, I spake as a child, I understood as a child, I thought as a child; but when I became a man, I put away childish things.

CHILDBIRTH
The Bible actually references a woman and how hard childbirth is, but what joy comes after the birth.
John 16:21: A woman when she is in travail hath sorrow, because her hour is come; but as soon as she is delivered of the child, she remembereth no more the anguish, for joy that a man is born into the world.

CHILREN-FEED FIRST
Mark 7:27: But Jesus said unto her, Let the children first be filled; for it is not meet to take the children's bread, and to cast it unto the dogs.

CHILDREN-JESUS' LOVE FOR THE CHILDREN
The Bible tells of Jesus' great love for the children.
Luke 9:47-48
Verse 47: And Jesus, perceiving the thought of their heart, took a child, and set him by him,
Verse 48: And said unto them, Whosoever shall

receive this child in my name receiveth me; and whosoever shall receive me receiveth him that sent me; for he that is least among you all, the same shall be great.

CHILDREN-NOT TO BE PROVOKED BY FATHERS
The Bible specifically tells fathers not to provoke their children.
Ephesians 6:4: And, ye fathers, provoke not your children to wrath; but bring them up in the nurture and admonition of the Lord.

COMPARING OURSELVES
II Corinthians 10:12: For we dare not make ourselves of the number, or compare ourselves with some that commend themselves; but they measuring themselves by themselves, and comparing themselves among themselves , are not wise.

CURSE OF THE LORD
Proverbs 3:33: The curse of the Lord is in the house of the wicked: but he blesseth the habitation of the just.

CURSING
The Bible says we should not curse.
Exodus 20:7: Thou shalt not take the name of the Lord thy God in vain; for the Lord will not hold him guiltless that taketh his name in vain.

CURSING - FATHER OR MOTHER
We should honor and respect our father and mothers.

Proverbs 20:20: Whoso curseth his father or his mother, his lamp shall be put out in obscure darkness.

DANCE
The Bible tells us about our emotions, it even tells us there is a time to dance.
Ecclesiastes 3:4: A time to weep, and a time to laugh; a time to mourn, and a time to dance.

DAVID - DANCED BEFORE THE LORD
Did you know David danced before the Lord?
II Samuel 6:14: And David danced before the Lord with all his might; and David was girded with a linen ephod.

DAYS-PROLONG THY DAYS UPON EARTH
Did you know that the Bible tells us that if we keep Christ's statutes and his commandments that our days will be prolonged upon this earth?
Deuteronomy 4:40: Thou shalt keep therefore his statutes, and his commandments, which I command thee this day, that it may go well with thee, and with thy children after thee, and that thou mayest prolong thy days upon the earth, which the Lord thy God giveth thee, for ever.

DEATH-THE DEAD SHALL LIVE AGAIN
The Bible tells us that those who believe in Christ will have life after death, a great promise.
John 5:24-29

Verse 24: Verily, verily, I say unto you, He that heareth my word, and believeth on him that sent me, hath everlasting life, and shall not come into condemnation; but is passed from death unto life.
Verse 25: Verily, verily, I say unto you, The hour is coming, and now is, when the dead shall hear the voice of the Son of God: and they that hear shall live.
Verse 26: For as the Father hath life in himself; so hath he given to the Son to have life in himself;
Verse 27: And hath given him authority to execute judgment also, because he is the Son of man.
Verse 28: Marvel not at this; for the hour is coming, in the which all that are in the graves shall hear his voice.
Verse 29: And shall come forth; they that have done good, unto the resurrection of life; and they that have done evil, unto the resurrection of damnation.

DEATH-AFTER THIS LIFE
Does this verse tell us that in heaven, no more of these things will exist?
Revelation 21:4: And God shall wipe away all tears from their eyes; and there shall be no more death, neither sorrow, nor crying, neither shall there be any more pain; for the former things are passed away.

DEVIL
Did you know the Bible tells us that the Devil wants to take God's word out of the hearts of Christians?
Luke 8:12: Those by the way side are they that hear; then cometh the devil, and taketh away the word out

of their hearts, lest they should believe and be saved.

DOORKEEPER

The Bible tells us in these verses that it is better to be in God's house than in the tents of wickedness.

Psalm 84:9-10:

Verse 9: Behold, O God our shield, and look upon the face of thine anointed.

Verse 10: For a day in thy courts is better than a thousand. I had rather be a doorkeeper in the house of my God, than to dwell in the tents of wickedness.

DUST-SHAKE THE DUST OFF YOUR FEET

Is the Bible telling us not to spend time with those who will not hear the Lord's words?

Matthew 10:13-14

Verse 13: And if the house be worthy, let your peace come upon it; but if it be not worthy, let your peace return to you.

Verse 14: And whosoever shall not receive you, nor hear your words, when ye depart out of that house or city, shake off the dust of your feet.

Mark 6:11: And whosoever shall not receive you, nor hear you, when ye depart thence, shake off the dust under your feet for a testimony against them. Verily I say unto you, It shall be more tolerable for Sodom and Gomorrha in the day of judgment, than for that city.

EARS-ITCHING EARS

Did you know the Bible talks about 'itching ears' and

how some will turn their ears away from the truth?
II Timothy 4:3-8

Verse 3: For the time will come when they will not endure sound doctrine; but after their own lusts shall they heap to themselves teachers, having itching ears.

Verse 4: And they shall turn away their ears from the truth, and shall be turned unto fables.

Verse 5: But watch thou in all things, endure afflictions, do the work of an evangelist, make full proof of thy ministry.

Verse 6: For I am now ready to be offered, and the time of my departure is at hand.

Verse 7: I have fought a good fight; I have finished my course; I have kept the faith.

Verse 8: Henceforth there is laid up for me a crown of righteousness, which the Lord, the righteous judge, shall give me at that day; and not to me only, but unto all them also that love his appearing.

EAST-THE SON OF MAN COMETH AGAIN OUT OF THE EAST

The Bible makes many, many references to the "EAST". This verse seems to indicate that when Christ comes again, it will be from the east.
Matthew 24:24-27

Verse 24: For there shall arise false Christs, and false prophets, and shall show great signs and wonders, insomuch that, if it were possible, they shall deceive the very elect.

Verse 25: Behold, I have told you before.

Verse 26: Wherefore if they shall say unto you,

Behold, he is in the desert; go not forth; behold, he is in the secret chambers; believe it not.

Verse 27: For as the lightning cometh out of the east, and shineth even unto the west; so shall also the coming of the Son of man be.

ELDERS

Is the Bible telling the young people to gather round the elders and learn from their wisdom?

I Peter 5:5: Likewise, ye younger, submit yourselves unto the elder. Yea, all of you be subject one to another, and be clothed with humility: for God resisteth the proud, and giveth grace to the humble.

James 5:14-15:

Verse 14: Is any sick among you? Let him call for the elders of the church; and let them pray over him, anointing him with oil in the name of the Lord.

Verse 15: And the prayer of faith shall save the sick, and the Lord shall raise him up; and if he have committed sins, they shall be forgiven him.

EVIL-WE SHOULD OVERCOME EVIL

The Bible admonishes us not to be overcome by the powerful forces, but struggle as hard as we can to overcome any evil.

Romans 12:21: Be not overcome of evil, but overcome evil with good.

Proverbs 3:7: Be not wise in thine own eyes; fear the Lord, and depart from evil.

EYES-THE EYES OF THE LORD ARE IN EVERY PLACE

Proverbs 15:3:   The eyes of the Lord are in every place, beholding the evil and the good.

Amos 9:8:   Behold, the eyes of the Lord God are upon the sinful kingdom, and I will destroy it from off the face of the earth; saving that I will not utterly destroy the house of Jacob, saith the Lord.

FACE-HIS NATURAL FACE IN A GLASS

Is this verse telling us to look in the mirror and not see ourselves and our ways, but to serve in the ways of our Lord, Jesus Christ?

James 1:23-24

Verse 23: For if any be a hearer of the word, and not a doer, he is like unto a man beholding his natural face in a glass.

Verse 24: For he beholdeth himself, and goeth his way, and straightway forgetteth what manner of man he was.

FAMILY-PROVIDING FOR YOUR FAMILY

The Bible tells us that we must provide for our own family.

I Timothy 5:8: But if any provide not for his own, and specially for those of his own house, he hath denied the faith, and is worse than an infidel.

Proverbs 23:22 Hearken unto thy father that begat

thee, and despise not thy mother when she is old.
*In this verse, isn't the Bible admonishing us to listen
to our Father and love and respect our Mother when
she is old:

FATHERLESS AND THE POOR
The Lord had great compassion for the fatherless,
afflicted, and the poor, and spoke often that they
should not be made fun of.
Psalm 82:3-4
Verse 3: Defend the poor and fatherless; do justice to
the afflicted and needy.
Verse 4: Deliver the poor and needy; rid them out of
the hand of the wicked.

FEAR OF THE LORD
This verse seems to tell us that all the world should
fear the Lord, for the power of Heaven is his.
Psalm 33:8: Let all the earth fear the Lord; let all the
inhabitants of the world stand in awe of him.
*This verse admonishes us to fear the Lord, study his
word, and gain wisdom. It says if we do so, our days
shall be multiplied and the years of our life will be
increased. What a great promise!

Proverbs 9:10-11
Verse 10: The fear of the Lord is the beginning of
wisdom; and the knowledge of the holy is
understanding.
Verse 11: For by me thy days shall be multiplied, and
the years of thy life shall be increased.

Proverbs 19:23: The fear of the Lord tendeth to life; and he that hath it shall abide satisfied; he shall not be visited with evil.

Proverbs 28:14: Happy is the man that feareth always: but he that hardeneth his heart shall fall into mischief.

FIERY DARTS OF THE WICKED
This verse tells us that if we take the shield of faith, we will be protected from the 'fiery darts' of the wicked.
Ephesians 6:16: Above all, taking the shield of faith, wherewith ye shall be able to quench all the fiery darts of the wicked.

FINGER- BIBLE IS WRITTEN BY THE FINGER OF GOD
These two verses indicate that the testimony of the Bible is true and was written with the finger of God.
Exodus 31:18   And he gave unto Moses, when he had made an end of communing with him upon mount Sinai, two tables of testimony, tables of stone, written with the finger of God.

Deuteronomy 9:10: And the Lord delivered unto me two tables of stone written with the finger of God; and on them was written according to all the words, which the Lord spake with you in the mount out of the midst of the fire in the day of the assembly.

GHOST

In two different chapters, the word 'ghost' appears (not the holy ghost) meaning Jesus died and gave up his life and spirit to God on the cross.

Matthew 27:50: Jesus, when he had cried again with a loud voice, yielded up the ghost.

Luke 23:46: And when Jesus had cried with a loud voice, he said, Father, into thy hands I commend my spirit; and having said thus, he gave up the ghost.

GIFTS-ALL GIFTS ARE FROM GOD

This verse tells us that everyone has different gifts given to them by the grace of God.

Romans 12:6: Having then gifts differing according to the grace that is given to us, whether prophecy, let us prophesy according to the proportion of faith.

James 1:17: Every good gift and every perfect gift is from above, and cometh down from the Father of lights, with whom is no variableness, neither shadow of turning.

GIFT GIVING-IN SECRET

Is God telling us we should not give just to be seen of men?

Matthew 6:1-4

Verse 1: TAKE HEED that ye do not your alms before men, to be seen of them; otherwise ye have no reward of your Father, which is in heaven.

Verse 2: Therefore when thou doest thine alms, do not sound a trumpet before thee, as the hypocrites do in the synagogues and in the streets, that they may have glory of men. Verily I say unto you; they have their reward.

Verse 3: But when thou doest alms, let not thy left hand know what thy right hand doeth.

Verse 4: That thine alms may be in secret; and thy Father which seeth in secret himself shall reward thee openly.

GIVING-MORE BLESSED TO GIVE

The Lord is telling us we will be more blessed by giving, rather than receiving, because there are those out there who are very poor and needy.

Acts 20:35: I have shown you all things, how that so labouring ye ought to support the weak, and to remember the words of the Lord Jesus, how he said, It is more blessed to give than to receive.

GOD-ANGRY WITH THE WICKED

A simple statement, but the Bible says:

Psalm 7:11: God judgeth the righteous, and God is angry with the wicked every day.

GOD-GOD'S WORD IS PURE

This verse tells us that God's word is pure, and He is our comforter.

Proverbs 30:5-6

Verse 5: Every word of God is pure; he is a shield unto them that put their trust in him.

Verse 6: Add thou not unto his words, lest he reprove thee, and thou be found a liar.

GOD-GOD CARES FOR YOU
Our God is a mighty God, but also a compassionate God who loves us.
I Peter 5:6-7
Verse 6: Humble yourselves therefore under the mighty hand of God, that he may exalt you in due time.
Verse 7: Casting all your care upon him; for he careth for you.

GOD-GOD KNOWS OUR EVERY THOUGHT
God knows our every thought, and we cannot withhold them from him.
Job 42:2: I know that thou canst do every thing, and that no thought can be withholden from thee.

GOD-SEEK GOD FIRST IN YOUR LIFE
If we trust in God and seek him first in our life, before all things, he will add many blessings upon us.
Matthew 6:33: But seek ye first the kingdom of God, and his righteousness; and all these things shall be added unto you.

HAIRS ON YOUR HEAD
Did you know the Bible tells us the hairs of our head are all numbered? How do you interpret this?
Matthew 10:30: But the very hairs of your head are all

numbered.

HAPPY

Doesn't this verse make you think that God does not want us to be TOO HARD on ourselves?

Romans 14:22: Hast thou faith? have it to thyself before God. Happy is he that condemneth not himself in that thing which he alloweth.

HATERS-THOSE WHO HATE YOU

As we go through life, there will ALWAYS be those who don't like us for one reason or another, this is just LIFE. We must remember that Jesus received the same treatment, even worse at times. Read Matthew, Mark, Luke and John for the torment Jesus went through for us.

John 15:18-20

Verse 18: If the world hate you, ye know that it hated me before it hated you.

Verse 19: If ye were of the world, the world would love his own; but because ye are not of the world, but I have chosen you out of the world, therefore the world hateth you.

Verse 20: Remember the word that I said unto you. The servant is not greater than his lord. If they have persecuted me, they will also persecute you; if they have kept my saying, they will keep yours also.

HEART-CREATE IN ME A CLEAN HEART

Is this verse telling us to change our lives, to be cleansed from sin from within; and asking God to give us his Holy Spirit as our comforter?

Psalm 51:10-11

Verse 10: Create in me a clean heart, O God; and renew a right spirit within me.

Verse 11: Cast me not away from thy presence; and take not thy holy spirit from me.

HEARTS-HARDENED HEARTS

The Bible speaks to us about fearing and trusting in the Lord always, but cautions us about the pitfalls of a hardened heart.

Proverbs 28:14: Happy is the man that feareth always; but he that hardeneth his heart shall fall into mischief.

HEARTS-MERRY HEARTS

Wow, another powerful Biblical statement. If we have a merry heart around others, it is contagious and a dose of 'good, happy medicine'.

Proverbs 17:22: A merry heart doeth good like a medicine; but a broken spirit drieth the bones.

HEART-A PROUD HEART

Is this verse telling us to keep our hearts pure, kind, and compassionate, as did our Lord Jesus Christ?

Proverbs 21:4: A high look, and a proud heart, and the plowing of the wicked, is sin.

Proverbs 28:25-27

Verse 25: He that is of a proud heart stirreth up strife; but he that putteth his trust in the Lord shall be made fat.

Verse 26: He that trusteth in his own heart is a fool; but whoso walketh wisely, he shall be delivered.

Verse 27: He that giveth unto the poor shall not lack; but he that hideth his eyes shall have many a curse.

HEAVEN-HEAVENLY MANSIONS
John 14:2-3

Verse 2: In my Father's house are many mansions; if it were not so, I would have told you. I go to prepare a place for you.

Verse 3: And if I go and prepare a place for you, I will come again, and receive you unto myself; that where I am, there ye may be also.

HIMSELF-MAN IS NOT TO THINK OF HIMSELF MORE HIGHLY THAN HE SHOULD
Romans 12:3: For I say, through the grace given unto me, to every man that is among you, not to think of himself more highly than he ought to think; but to think soberly, according as God hath dealt to every man the measure of faith.

IMAGE-GOD MADE MAN IN HIS OWN IMAGE
This verse is awesome; it tells us that we are in the very image of God and Jesus.

Genesis 1:26-27

Verse 26: And God said, Let us make man in our image, after our likeness; and let them have dominion over the fish of the sea, and over the fowl of the air, and over the cattle, and over all the earth, and over

every creeping thing that creepeth upon the earth.
Verse 27: So God created man in his own image, in the image of God created he him; male and female created he them.

IMPOSSIBLE THINGS
In Jesus' own words, our Lord is telling us that all things are possible if we believe in God.
Luke 18:27: And he said, The things which are impossible with men are possible with God.

INIQUITY (SIN)
This verse teaches us that God expects us to turn away from sin, serve him, and keep his commandments.
Job 36:10-12
Verse 10: He openeth also their ear to discipline, and commandeth that they return from iniquity.
Verse 11: If they obey and serve him, they shall spend their days in prosperity, and their years in pleasures.
Verse 12: But if they obey not, they shall perish by the sword, and they shall die without knowledge.

INSTRUMENTS
The Bible speaks many, many times about musical instruments for the glorification of God.
Psalm 87:7: As well the singers as the players on instruments shall be there; all my springs are in thee.
Psalm 92:3: Upon an instrument of ten strings, and upon the psaltery; upon the harp with a solemn

sound.

Psalm 144:9:   I will sing a new song unto thee, O God; upon a psaltery and an instrument of ten strings will I sing praises unto thee.

INTEGRITY (HONESTY)

These three verses seem to tell us that the Lord expects us to be honest and exhibit righteousness, for we know we will be judged by the Lord according to our actions and deeds someday.

Psalm 7:8: The Lord shall judge the people; judge me, O Lord, according to my righteousness, and according to mine integrity that is in me.

Proverbs 11:3-4

Verse 3: The integrity of the upright shall guide them; but he perverseness of transgressors shall destroy them.

Verse 4: Riches profit not in the day of wrath; but righteousness delivereth from death.

IRON PEN

Did you know that Job's words were printed in a book, and written with an iron pen?

Job 19:23-24

Verse 23: Oh that my words were now written! oh that they were printed in a book!

Verse 24: That they were graven with an iron pen and

lead in the rock for ever!

JESUS-WAITING ON JESUS

These verses tell us to watch and wait for Jesus' second coming. Jesus asks us to have our hearts right with God, for no man knows the day or hour that he will come.

Mark 13:32-33

Verse 32: But of that day and that hour knoweth no man; no, not the angels which are in heaven; neither the Son, but the Father.

Verse 33: Take ye heed, watch and pray; for ye know not when the time is.

Mark 13:35: Watch ye therefore; for ye know not when the master of the house cometh, at even, or at midnight, or at the cockcrowing, or in the morning.

I Peter 4:7: But the end of all things is at hand; be ye therefore sober, and watch unto prayer.

JESUS-WILL NEVER LEAVE US COMFORTLESS

Doesn't this verse tell us Jesus will never leave us alone; he will always be there to comfort us?

John 14:18: I will not leave you comfortless; I will come to you.

JESUS-FAR FROM THE WICKED

This verse is clear, and Jesus hears all the prayers of the righteous.

<u>Proverbs 15:29</u>: The Lord is far from the wicked; but he heareth the prayer of the righteous.

JESUS-JESUS DOES GOD'S WILL
By Jesus' example, he is admonishing us to do God's will.
<u>John 6:38</u>: For I came down from heaven, not to do mine own will, but the will of him that sent me.

JESUS-JESUS IS FROM HEAVEN
In Jesus' own words, He tells us He was sent down to earth from Heaven.
<u>John 8:23</u>: And he said unto them, Ye are from beneath; I am from above; ye are of this world; I am not of this world.

JESUS-JESUS WEPT
Crying is normal emotion. Our Lord was so compassionate for Mary's loss of her brother that he wept with her.
<u>John 11:32-35 & Verses 43-44</u>
<u>Verse 32</u>: Then when Mary was come where Jesus was, and saw him, she fell down at his feet; saying unto him, Lord, if thou hadst been here, my brother had not died.
<u>Verse 33</u>: When Jesus therefore saw her weeping, and the Jews also weeping which came with her, he groaned in the spirit, and was troubled.
<u>Verse 34</u>: And said, Where have ye laid him? They said unto him, Lord, come and see.
<u>Verse 35</u>: Jesus wept.

Verse 43: And when he thus had spoken, he cried with a loud voice, Lazarus, come forth.

Verse 44: And he that was dead came forth, bound hand and foot with graveclothes; and his face was bound about with a napkin. Jesus saith unto them, Loose him, and let him go.

JESUS' SECOND COMING-HE'LL COME OUT OF THE EAST

In Jesus' own words, He gives us this scripture about his second coming.

Matthew 24:27: For as the lightning cometh out of the east, and shineth even unto the west; so shall also the coming of the Son of man be.

Revelation 22:7: Behold, I come quickly; blessed is he that keepeth the sayings of the prophecy of this book.

JOY-NO GREATER JOY

What a powerful statement!

III John 4: I have no greater joy than to hear that my children walk in truth.

JUDGMENT-EVERY SECRET THING

At the Judgment Day, God will know every good and evil thing we have done.

Ecclesiastes 12:14: For God shall bring every work into judgment, with every secret thing; whether it be good, or whether it be evil.

KEEPING HIS COMMANDMENTS

It is the Lord's desire that we keep his commandments.

John 14:15: If ye love me, keep my commandments.

KINGDOM-SEEK YE FIRST THE KINGDOM OF GOD

See how blessed we will be if we put God first in our lives?

Matthew 6:33: But seek ye first the kingdom of God, and his righteousness; and all these things shall be added unto you.

Luke 12:29-31

Verse 29: And seek not ye what ye shall eat, or what ye shall drink, neither be ye of doubtful mind.

Verse 30: For all these things do the nations of the world seek after; and your Father knoweth that ye have need of these things.

Verse 31: But rather seek ye the kingdom of God; and all these things shall be added unto you.

KISS-GREET ONE ANOTHER WITH A HOLY KISS

Is the Bible telling us to love one another with the love of Jesus?

I Corinthians 16:20: All the brethren greet you. Greet ye one another with an holy kiss.

II Corinthians 13:12: Greet one another with an holy kiss.

KEEPING JESUS' COMMANDMENTS
There are many, many verses in the Bible that tell us we should keep Jesus' commandments
Revelation 2:26: And he that overcometh and keepeth my works unto the end, to him will I give power over the nations.
Revelation 22:7: Behold, I come quickly: blessed is he that keepeth the sayings of the prophecy of this book.

KEEPING JESUS' COMMANDMENTS
Revelation 3:10: Because thou hast kept the word of my patience, I also will keep thee from the hour of temptation, which shall come upon all the world, to try them that dwell upon the earth.
Revelation 14:12-13
Verse 12: Here is the patience of the saints: here are they that keep the commandments of God, and the faith of Jesus.
Verse 13: And I heard a voice from heaven saying unto me, Write, Blessed are the dead which die in the Lord from henceforth: Yea, saith the Spirit, that they may rest from their labours; and their works do follow them.
Revelation 22:9-12
Verse 9: Then saith he unto me, See thou do it not, for I am thy fellowservant, and of thy brethren the

prophets, and of them which keep the sayings of this book: worship God.

Verse 10: And he saith unto me, Seal not the sayings of the prophecy of this book: for the time is at hand.

Verse 11: He that is unjust, let him be unjust still, and he which is filthy, let him be filthy still: and he that is righteous, let him be righteous still: and he that is holy, let him be holy still.

Verse 12: And, behold, I come quickly; and my reward is with me, to give every man according as his work shall be.

KEEPERS OF THE HOME-YOUNG WOMEN

These verses stress that younger women should learn from the aged women.

Titus 2:3-5

Verse 3: The aged women likewise, that they be in behaviour as becometh holiness, not false accusers, not given to much wine, teachers of good things.

Verse 4: That they may teach the young women to be sober, to love their husbands, to love their children.

LABOR-MEN AND WOMEN WHO WORK

God tells us in these three verses that it is good to work, two people working are better than one, and our jobs are from the hand of God.

Ecclesiastes 2:24: There is nothing better for a man, than that he should eat and drink, and that he should make his soul enjoy good in his labour. This also I saw, that it was from the hand of God.

Ecclesiastes 3:13: And also that every man should eat

and drink, and enjoy the good of all his labour, it is the gift of God.

Ecclesiastes 4:9-10
Verse 9: Two are better than one; because they have a good reward for their labour.
Verse 10: For if they fall, the one will lift up his fellow; but woe to him that is alone when he falleth, for he hath not another to help him up.

LAST DAYS-THE SECOND COMING OF CHRIST
These verses give the signs of the last days before Jesus comes.
Mark 13:7-11
Verse 7: And when ye shall hear of wars and rumours of wars, be ye not troubled: for such things must needs be; but the end shall not be yet.
Verse 8: For nation shall rise against nation, and kingdom against kingdom: and there shall be earthquakes in divers places, and there shall be famines and troubles: these are the beginnings of sorrows.
Verse 9: But take heed to yourselves: for they shall deliver you up to councils; and in the synagogues ye shall be beaten: and ye shall be brought before rulers and kings for my sake, for a testimony against them.
Verse 10: And the gospel must first be published among all nations.
Verse 11: But when they shall lead you, and deliver you up, take no thought beforehand what ye shall

speak, neither do ye premeditate; but whatsoever shall be given you in that hour, that speak ye; for it is not ye that speak, but the Holy Ghost.

LAUGHTER
Did you know the Bible often talked about laughter?
<u>Psalm 2:4</u>: He that sitteth in the heavens shall laugh: the Lord shall have them in derision.
<u>Psalm 37:13</u>: The Lord shall laugh at him: for he seeth that his day is coming.
<u>Psalm 52:6</u>: The righteous also shall see, and fear, and shall laugh at him.
<u>Psalm 59:8</u>: But thou, O Lord, shalt laugh at them; thou shalt have all the heathen in derision.

<u>Job 5:22</u>: At destruction and famine thou shalt laugh: neither shalt thou be afraid of the beasts of the earth.
<u>Job 9:23</u>: If the scourge slay suddenly; he will laugh at the trial of the innocent.
<u>Job 29:24</u>: If I laughed on them, they believed it not; and the light of my countenance they cast not down.
<u>Job 41:29</u>: Darts are counted as stubble: he laugheth at the shaking of a spear.

LENDING
This verse tells us to love everyone, do good, and to lend to those who need help, without hoping for anything in return.
<u>Luke 6:35</u>: But love ye your enemies, and do good, and lend, hoping for nothing again; and your reward shall be great, and ye shall be the children of the

Highest: for he is kind unto the unthankful and to the evil.

LIFE AFTER DEATH
Doesn't this verse tell us of the life which is to come?
I Timothy 4:8: For bodily exercise profiteth little: but godliness is profitable unto all things, having promise of the life that now is, and of that which is to come.

LYING LIPS
Did you know the Bible speaks of "lying lips"?
Psalm 31:18: Let the lying lips be put to silence; which speak grievous things proudly and contemptuously against the righteous.

MAGICIANS
Did you know the Bible talks about the magicians of Egypt?
Genesis 41:8: And it came to pass in the morning that his spirit was troubled; and he sent and called for all the magicians of Egypt, and all the wise men thereof; and Pharaoh told them his dream; but there was none that could interpret them unto Pharaoh.

MAN-THE SPIRIT OF MAN GOETH UPWARD
What do you perceive this verse to mean?
Ecclesiastes 3:21: Who knoweth the spirit of man that goeth upward, and the spirit of the beast that goeth downward to the earth?

MANNERS-MANNERS OF A HEATHEN
What is the Bible telling us about keeping company with those who walk in the heathen way?
Ezekiel 11:12: And ye shall know that I am the Lord: for ye have not walked in my statutes, neither executed my judgments, but have done after the manners of the heathen that are round about you.

MANY OCCUPATIONS
Isn't it amazing that the Bibles speaks of many of our occupations used today?
Ezekiel 27:27: Thy riches, and thy fairs, thy merchandise, thy mariners, and thy pilots, thy calkers, and the occupiers of thy merchandise, and all thy men of war, that are in thee, and in all thy company which is in the midst of thee, shall fall into the midst of the seas in the day of thy ruin.

MEEK-SHALL INHERIT THE EARTH
Doesn't this scripture tell us that the righteous servants of God, the meek and humble, shall inherit the earth?
Psalm 37:11: But the meek shall inherit the earth; and shall delight themselves in the abundance of peace.

MEN-MEAN MEN
What is the Bible trying to tell us about mean men

(and perhaps mean women)?

Isaiah 5:15: And the mean man shall be brought down, and the mighty man shall be humbled, and the eyes of the lofty shall be humbled.

MEN-WALKING WITH WISE MEN

Is the Bible telling us not to walk with foolish people?

Proverbs 13:20: He that walketh with wise men shall be wise: but a companion of fools shall be destroyed.

Proverbs 14:16: A wise man feareth, and departeth from evil: but the fool rageth, and is confident.

MEN-YOUNG MEN

The Bible tells young men to be sober minded, do good work, and be honest.

Titus 2:6-7

Verse 6: Young men likewise exhort to be sober minded.

Verse 7: In all things showing thyself a pattern of good works, in doctrine showing uncorruptness, gravity, sincerity.

MIRACLES-JESUS PERFORMED MIRACLES

Jesus performed many miracles of healing and showed wonders and signs, the mighty Son of God.

Acts 2:22: Ye men of Israel, hear these words; Jesus of Nazareth, a man approved of God among you by miracles and wonders and signs, which God did by him in the midst of you, as ye yourselves also know.

MOURNING

We will never be left alone in our time of mourning.

Matthew 5:4: Blessed are they that mourn: for they shall be comforted.

NETWORK-NETWORK OF POMEGRANATES
Did you know that there was a network of pomegranates, and pomegranates were mentioned a lot in the Bible?
Jeremiah 52:23: And there were ninety and six pomegranates on a side; and all the pomegranates upon the network were an hundred round about.

NON-BELIEVERS- JESUS SPOKE OF THE NON-BELIEVERS
Jesus knew Thomas did not believe that He rose on the third day. Does this same point echo today with some non-believers? If they can't see Jesus, it is hard for them to believe?
John 20:27-29
Verse 27: Then saith he to Thomas, Reach hither thy finger, and behold my hands; and reach hither thy hand, and thrust it into my side; and be not faithless, but believing.
Verse 28: And Thomas answered and said unto him, My Lord and my God.
Verse 29: Jesus saith unto him, Thomas, because thou hast seen me, thou hast believed; blessed are they that have not seen; and yet have believed.

NON-BELIEVERS-SHAKE THE DUST OFF YOUR FEET
Is Jesus speaking of those who would not listen to

His disciples who were trying to spread the gospel?
Matthew 10:13-14
Verse 13: And if the house be worthy, let your peace

come upon it; but if it be not worthy, let your peace
return to you.
Verse 14: And whosoever shall not receive you, nor
hear your words, when ye depart out of that house or
city, shake off the dust of your feet.

OIL- ANOINTING OIL

The Bible references anointing oil many times.
Exodus 40:9: And thou shalt take the anointing oil,
and anoint the tabernacle, and all that is therein, and
shalt hallow it, and all the vessels thereof; and it shall
be holy.

James 5:14: Is any sick among you? Let him call for
the elders of the church; and let them pray over him,
anointing him with oil in the name of the Lord.

Leviticus 8:2: Take Aaron and his sons with him, and
the garments, and the anointing oil, and a bullock for
the sin offering, and two rams, and a basket of
unleavened bread.
Leviticus 8:10: And Moses took the anointing oil, and
anointed the tabernacle and all that was therein, and
sanctified them.
Leviticus 8:12: And he poured of the anointing oil
upon Aaron's head, and anointed him, to sanctify
him.

OLDER PEOPLE

The Bible tells us that when we get old, we will have special needs.

John 21:18: Verily, verily, I say unto thee, When thou wast young, thou girdest thyself, and walkedst whither thou wouldest; but when thou shalt be old, thou shalt stretch forth thy hands, and another shall gird thee, and carry thee whither thou wouldest not.

OSTRICH AND PEACOCKS IN THE BIBLE

Job 39:13: Gavest thou the goodly wings unto the peacocks? or wings and feathers unto the ostrich?

OWNER RESPONSIBILITY

Isn't this an example of Christian righteousness?

Exodus 21:33-34

Verse 33: And if a man shall open a pit, or if a man shall dig a pit, and not cover it; and an ox or an ass fall therein.

Verse 34: The owner of the pit shall make it good; and give money unto the owner of them; and the dead beast shall be his.

PARABLE-OF ONE LOST SHEEP

It seems this verse is telling us Jesus loves all of us, and one person lost to sin is important to him. It tells us that there is joy in heaven over one sinner that repented.

Luke 15:3-7

Verse 3: And he spake this parable unto them,

saying,

Verse 4: What man of you, having an hundred sheep, if he lose one of them, doth not leave the ninety and nine in the wilderness, and go after that which is lost, until he finds it?

Verse 5: And when he hath found it; he layeth it on his shoulders, rejoicing.

Verse 6: And when he cometh home, he calleth together his friends and neighbors, saying unto them, Rejoice with me; for I have found my sheep which was lost.

Verse 7: I say unto you, that likewise joy shall be in heaven over one sinner that repenteth, more than over ninety and nine just persons, which need no repentance.

PAVEMENT

Did you know that way back in Biblical days, the Bible tells us there was 'pavement', not just dirt streets?

Ezekiel 40:17-18

Verse 17: Then brought he me into the outward court, and, lo, there were chambers, and a pavement made for the court round about: thirty chambers were upon the pavement.

Verse 18: And the pavement by the side of the gates over against the length of the gates was the lower pavement.

PEACEMAKERS

Doesn't this verse ask us to be peaceful people,

promising that we will be called God's children?
Matthew 5:9: Blessed are the peacemakers: for they shall be called the children of God.

PERSECUTION
Is this verse telling us that if Christian believers are persecuted for Christ's sake that they will be in heaven some day?
Matthew 5:10: Blessed are they which are persecuted for righteousness' sake: for theirs is the kingdom of heaven.

POETS
Did you know the Bible speaks of POETS?
Acts 17:28: For in him we live, and move, and have our being; as certain also of your own poets have said, For we are also his offspring.

POMEGRANATE TREES-OTHER HEALTHY THINGS
Does this verse tell us that everything is a 'gift from God' and that we should be thankful for all our blessings from him?
Deuteronomy 8:7-10
Verse 7: For the Lord thy God bringeth thee into a good land, a land of brooks of water, of fountains and depths that spring out of valleys and hills.
Verse 8: A land of wheat, and barley, and vines, and fig trees, and pomegranates; a land of oil olive, and honey.

Verse 9: A land wherein thou shalt eat bread without scarceness, thou shall not lack any thing in it; a land whose stones are iron, and out of whose hills thou mayest dig brass.

Verse 10: When thou hast eaten and art full, then thou shalt bless the Lord thy God for the good land which he hath given thee.

POOR-THE CRY OF THE POOR

There are many, many verses that admonish us to have compassion for the poor and to help them unreservedly.

Proverbs 21:13: Whoso stoppeth his ears at the cry of the poor, he also shall cry himself, but shall not be heard.

Proverbs 22:9: He that hath a bountiful eye shall be blessed; for he giveth of his bread to the poor.

Psalm 35:10: All my bones shall say, Lord, who is like unto thee, which deliverest the poor from him that is too strong for him, yea, the poor and the needy from him that spoileth him?

POOR-MOCKING THE POOR

Doesn't this scripture tell us that those who mock the poor angers his Heavenly Father and will be punished?

Proverbs 17:5: Whoso mocketh the poor reproacheth his Maker: and he that is glad at calamities shall not be unpunished.

QUAILS

Did you know that quails were a source of food in Biblical times?

Numbers 11:32: And the people stood up all that day, and all that night, and all the next day, and they gathered the quails; he that gathered least gathered ten homers: and they spread them all abroad for themselves round about the camp.

QUEEN OF THE SOUTH

How do you interpret this verse?

Luke 11:31: The queen of the south shall rise up in the judgment with the men of this generation, and condemn them: for she came from the utmost parts of the earth to hear the wisdom of Solomon; and, behold, a greater than Solomon is here.

RAINBOWS

Did you know the Bible talks about RAINBOWS?

Revelation 4:1-3

Verse 1: After this I looked, and, behold, a door was opened in heaven: and the first voice which I heard was as it were of a trumpet talking with me; which said, Come up hither, and I will show thee things which must be hereafter.

Verse 2: And immediately I was in the spirit; and, behold, a throne was set in heaven, and one sat on the throne.

Verse 3: And he that sat was to look upon like a jasper and a sardine stone: and there was a rainbow

round about the throne, in sight like unto an emerald.
Revelation 10:1: And I saw another mighty angel
come down from heaven, clothed with a cloud: and a
rainbow was upon his head, and his face was as it
were the sun, and his feet as pillars of fire.

RECEIVING-PRAYERS-RECEIVING BLESSINGS

Isn't this verse telling us that if we pray asking the
Lord for something in our life that we will receive it,
that is, is we BELIEVE that we shall receive it? We
never know in what time frame we will receive our
blessings, but we will receive them.
Mark 11:24: Therefore I say unto you, What things
soever ye desire, when ye pray, believe that ye receive
them, and ye shall have them.

REJOICE IN THE LORD

The Lord is our salvation, and he will have joy over
us with singing, what a beautiful promise.
Habakkuk 3:18-19
Verse 18: Yet I will rejoice in the Lord, I will joy in the
God of my salvation.
Verse 19: The Lord God is my strength, and he will
make my feet like hinds' feet, and he will make me to
walk upon mine high places. To the chief singer on
my stringed instruments.

Zephaniah 3:17: The Lord thy God in the midst of
thee is mighty; he will save, he will rejoice over thee
with joy; he will rest in his love, he will joy over thee
with singing.

REPENTANCE-GOD WINKED

Did you know in this verse the Bible said God 'WINKED"?

Acts 17:30-31

Verse 30: And the times of this ignorance God winked at; but now commandeth all men everywhere to repent.

Verse 31: Because he hath appointed a day, in the which he will judge the world in righteousness by that man whom he hath ordained; whereof he hath given assurance unto all men, in that he hath raised him from the dead.

RESPECT

This verse says it all about respecting others.

I Timothy 5:1-4

Verse 1: Rebuke not an elder, but entreat him as a father; and the younger men as brethren.

Verse 2: The elder women as mothers, the younger as sisters, with all purity.

Verse 3: Honour widows that are widows indeed.

Verse 4: But if any widow have children or nephews, let them learn first to show piety at home, and to requite their parents: for that is good and acceptable before God.

SAMARITAN, THE GOOD SAMARITAN

Aren't we bound by Jesus' example to be good Samaritans of our fellow men?

Luke 10:30-35

<u>Verse 30</u>: And Jesus answering said, A certain man went down from Jerusalem to Jericho, and fell among thieves, which stripped him of his raiment, and wounded him, and departed, leaving him half dead.

<u>Verse 31</u>: And by chance there came down a certain priest that way; and when he saw him, he passed by on the other side.

<u>Verse 32</u>: And likewise a Levite, when he was at the place, came and looked on him, and passed by on the other side.

<u>Verse 33</u>: But a certain Samaritan, as he journeyed, came where he was; and when he saw him, he had compassion on him.

<u>Verse 34</u>: And went to him, and bound up his wounds, pouring in oil and wine, and set him on his own beast, and brought him to an inn, and took care of him.

<u>Verse 35</u>: And on the morrow when he departed, he took out two pence, and gave them to the host, and said unto him, Take care of him; and whatsoever thou spendest more, when I come again, I will repay thee.

SATAN-GET THEE BEHIND ME SATAN

How many times have we heard this famous Biblical saying? It is true, Satan wants us to be sinful and seek the ways of men, rather than be saved and be Christians.

<u>Matthew 16:23</u>: But he turned, and said unto Peter, Get thee behind me, Satan: thou art an offence unto me: for thou savourest not the things that be of God, but those that be of men.

SAVED-BEING BORN AGAIN

Jesus tells us that unless we accept him and are saved, we will not enter into the kingdom of Heaven

John 3:5: Jesus answered, Verily, verily, I say unto thee, Except a man be born of water and of the Spirit, he cannot enter into the kingdom of God.

SAVED-BY HOPE

Does this verse tell us to believe in Jesus with hope, even though he has ascended to Heaven?

Romans 8:24-25

Verse 24: For we are saved by hope: but hope that is seen is not hope: for what a man seeth, why doth he yet hope for?

Verse 25: But if we hope for that we see not, then do we with patience wait for it.

SAVED-HOW TO BE SAVED

This verse tells us how to be saved.

Romans 10:9-10

Verse 9: That if thou shalt confess with thy mouth the Lord Jesus, and shall believe in thine heart that God hath raised him from the dead, thou shalt be saved.

Verse 10: For with the heart man believeth unto righteousness; and with the mouth confession is made unto salvation.

SCRIPTURES-INSPIRATION OF GOD

Did you know the Bible tells us that the scriptures were the inspiration of God?

II Timothy 3:16-17

Verse 16: All scripture is given by inspiration of God, and is profitable for doctrine, for reproof, for correction, for instruction in righteousness.

Verse 17: That the man of God may be perfect, thoroughly furnished unto all good works.

SHIP-SAILING SHIP CONSTRUCTION DESCRIBED

Ezekiel 27:5-9

Verse 5: They have made all thy ship boards of fir trees of Senir: they have taken cedars from Lebanon to make masts for thee.

Verse 6: Of the oaks of Bashan have they made thine oars; the company of the Ashurites have made thy benches of ivory, brought out of the Isles of Chittim.

Verse 7: Fine linen with broidered work from Egypt was that which thou spreadest forth to be thy sail; blue and purple from the isles of Elishah was that which covered thee.

Verse 8: The inhabitants of Zidon and Arvad were thy mariners: thy wise men, O Tyrus, that were in thee, were thy pilots.

Verse 9: The ancients of Gebal and the wise men thereof were in thee thy calkers; all the ships of the sea with their mariners were in thee to occupy thy merchandise.

TABLE-TABLE OF DEVILS

Is this verse telling us that we cannot be 'part-time' Christians?

I Corinthians 10:21: Ye cannot drink the cup of the Lord, and the cup of devils: ye cannot be partakers of the Lord's table, and of the table of devils.

TALEBEARERS (GOSSIPERS)

Isn't this good advice for us today, realizing that Jesus does not want us to spread tales about people?
Proverbs 11:13-15
Verse 13: A talebearer revealeth secrets: but he that is of a faithful spirit concealeth the matter.
Verse 14: Where no counsel is, the people fall: but in the multitude of counsellors there is safety.
Verse 15: He that is surety for a stranger shall smart for it: and he that hateth suretyship is sure.
Proverbs 20:19: He that goeth about as a talebearer revealeth secrets: therefore meddle not with him that flattereth with his lips.

TEACHING-TEACHING CHILDREN GOD'S WORDS

Aren't these verses telling us that we should teach our children about Jesus and the Bible?
Deuteronomy 11:18-19
Verse 18: Therefore shall ye lay up these my words in your heart and in your soul, and bind them for a sign upon your hand, that they may be as frontlets between your eyes.
Verse 19: And ye shall teach them your children, speaking of them when thou sittest in thine house, and when thou walkest by the way, when thou liest

down, and when thou risest up.

TENDERHEARTED
This verse tells us what Jesus expects of us.
Ephesians 4:32: And be ye kind one to another, tenderhearted, forgiving one another, even as God for Christ's sake hath forgiven you.

THUNDERBOLTS-HOT THUNDERBOLTS
Did you know the Bible speaks of 'hot thunderbolts"?
Psalm 78:48: He gave up their cattle also to the hail, and their flocks to hot thunderbolts.

TIRES-TIRES SHALL BE UPON YOUR HEADS
Did you know the Bible actually speaks about 'TIRES', and tires upon your head?
Ezekiel 24:23: And your tires shall be upon your heads, and your shoes upon your feet; ye shall not mourn nor weep; but ye shall pine away for your iniquities, and mourn one toward another.

TONGUE-TEACH ME TO HOLD MY TONGUE
Did you know the Bible tells us to 'hold our tongues'?
Job 6:24-25
Verse 24: Teach me, and I will hold my tongue: and cause me to understand wherein I have erred.
Verse 25: How forcible are right words! but what doth your arguing reprove?

TRIBULATIONS

Doesn't this verse tell us that we will have problems in life, but they will be overcome through our Lord Jesus Christ?

John 16:33: These things I have spoken unto you, that in me ye might have peace. In the world ye shall have
Tribulation: but be of good cheer; I have overcome the world.

UNBELIEVERS

Did you know the Bible is very clear regarding people who are unbelievers?

Titus 1:15-16

Verse 15: Unto the pure all things are pure: but unto them that are defiled and unbelieving is nothing pure; but even their mind and conscience is defiled.

Verse 16: They profess that they know God; but in works they deny him, being abominable, and disobedient, and unto every good work reprobate.

UNICORNS-THE BIBLE SPEAKS OF UNICORNS

Yes, the Bible actually speaks about UNICORNS.
Did you know?

Job 39:9-10

Verse 9: Will the unicorn be willing to serve thee, or

abide by thy crib?

Verse 10: Canst thou bind the unicorn with his band in the furrow? Or will he harrow the valleys after thee?

Psalm 22:21: Save me from the lion's mouth: for thou hast heard me from the horns of the unicorns.
Psalm 92:10: But my horn shalt thou exalt like the horn of an unicorn; I shall be anointed with fresh oil.

Numbers 24:8:   God brought him forth out of Egypt; he hath as it were the strength of an unicorn: he shall eat up the nations his enemies, and shall break their bones, and pierce them through with his arrows.

UNWORTHINESS-THE CENTURION'S GREAT STORY
Luke 7:2-10

Verse 2: And a certain centurion's servant, who was dear unto him, was sick, and ready to die.

Verse 3: And when he heard of Jesus, he sent unto him the elders of the Jews, beseeching him that he would come and heal his servant.

Verse 4: And when they came to Jesus, they besought him instantly, saying, That he was worthy for whom he should do this.

Verse 5: For he loveth our nation, and he hath built us a synagogue.

Verse 6: Then Jesus went with them. And when he was now not far from the house, the centurion sent friends to him, saying unto him, Lord, trouble not thyself; for I am not worthy that thou shouldest enter under my roof.

Verse 7: Wherefore neither thought I myself worthy to come unto thee; but say in a word, and my servant shall be healed.

Verse 8: For I also am a man set under authority, having under me soldiers, and I say unto one, Go, and he goeth; and to another, Come, and he cometh; and to my servant, Do this, and he doeth it.

Verse 9: When Jesus heard these things, he marvelled at him, and turned him about, and said unto the people that followed him, I say unto you, I have not found so great faith, no, not in Israel.

Verse 10: And they that were sent, returning to the house, found the servant whole that had been sick.

VINEGAR

Did you know the Bible speaks of vinegar, and that it was given to Jesus on the cross? It was the last thing our Savior had to drink.

John 19:30: When Jesus therefore had received the vinegar, he said, It is finished: and he bowed his head, and gave up the ghost.

WALK-WALK IN LOVE

Doesn't this verse tell us to be followers of God and exhibit love for one another, as Christ did for us?

Ephesians 5:1-2

Verse 1: BE YE therefore followers of God, as dear children.

Verse 2: And walk in love, as Christ also hath loved us, and hath given himself for us an offering and a sacrifice to God for a sweetsmelling savour.

WARS AND RUMORS OF WARS

Isn't this verse telling us the signs of the last days, but that believers should not be terrified of these things that must come about?

Luke 21:9-11

Verse 9: But when ye shall hear of wars and commotions, be not terrified; for these things must first come to pass; but the end is not by and by.

Verse 10: Then said he unto them, Nation shall rise against nation, and kingdom against kingdom.

Verse 11: And great earthquakes shall be in divers places, and famines, and pestilences, and fearful sights and great signs shall there be from heaven.

WASH-BE BAPTIZED AND WASH AWAY YOUR SINS

For those who call upon the name of the Lord, what a beautiful gift he gives us, the cleansing of our sins.

Acts 22:16: And now why tarriest thou? arise, and be baptized, and wash away thy sins, calling on the name of the Lord.

WASH-JESUS WASHED THE DISCIPLES FEET

Wow! Look at the humbleness of our Lord? He is our Savior, he didn't have to wash his disciples' feet, but he did.

John 13:5: After that he poureth water into a basin, and began to wash the disciples' feet, and to wipe them with the towel wherewith he was girded.

WASH-WASHED MY STEPS WITH BUTTER

Did you know there is a Bible verse that talks about 'washing his steps with butter'?

Job 29:6: When I washed my steps with butter, and the rock poured me out rivers of oil.

WAYS OF MAN

Isn't this verse telling us that we cannot hide our ways
or our sins from the Lord God?

Jeremiah 16:17: For mine eyes are upon all their ways; they are not hid from my face, neither is their iniquity hid from mine eyes.

WEEP

The Bible is telling us to be compassionate, minding not high things, and to not be wise in our own conceits.

Romans 12:15-16

Verse 15: Rejoice with them that do rejoice, and weep with them that weep.

Verse 16: Be of the same mind one toward another. Mind not high things, but condescend to men of low estate. Be not wise in your own conceits.

YEARS-YOUR YEARS PROLONGED

Doesn't this verse say it all? If we live for the Lord, our years will be increased.

Proverbs 9:10-11

Verse 10: The fear of the Lord is the beginning of wisdom: and the knowledge of the holy is understanding.

Verse 11: For by me thy days shall be multiplied, and the years of thy life shall be increased.

YOUNG

The young are admonished to help the old.

John 21:18: Verily, verily, I say unto thee, When thou wast young, thou girdest thyself, and walkedst whither thou wouldest: but when thou shalt be old, thou shalt stretch forth thy hands, and another shall gird thee, and carry thee whither thou wouldest not.

YOUNG MEN

Titus 2:6: Young men likewise exhort to be sober minded.

YOUTHFUL THOUGHTS

II Timothy 2:22-23

Verse 22: Flee also youthful lust: but follow righteousness, faith, charity, peace, with them that call on the Lord out of a pure heart.

Verse 23: But foolish and unlearned questions avoid, knowing that they do gender strifes.

YOUR WAYS

Isn't this the Bible telling us to consider our ways and telling us how to conduct our lives?
Haggai 1:5-7
Verse 5: Now therefore thus saith the Lord of hosts; Consider your ways.

Verse 6: Ye have sown much, and bring in little; ye eat, but ye have not enough; ye drink, but ye are not filled with drink; ye clothe you, but there is none warm; and he that earneth wages earneth wages, to put it into a bag with holes.
Verse 7: Thus saith the Lord of hosts; Consider your ways.

ZION-MOUNT ZION, A HOLY HILL

Mount Zion is described below as a very special place, a HOLY HILL.
Psalm 2:6: Yet have I set my king upon my holy hill of Zion.
Psalm 48:2: Beautiful for situation, the joy of the whole earth, is mount Zion, on the sides of the north, the city of the great King.

Isaiah 60:14: The sons also of them that afflicted thee shall come bending unto thee; and all they that despised thee shall bow themselves down at the soles of thy feet; and they shall call thee, The city of the Lord, The Zion of the Holy One of Israel.

Hebrews 12:22: But ye are come unto mount Zion,

and unto the city of the living God, the heavenly
Jerusalem, and to an innumerable company of angels.

GOD CARES FOR YOU AND HE DESIRES TO TAKE CARE OF YOU

<u>Luke 12:22-31</u>
<u>Verse 22:</u> And he said unto his disciples,
Therefore, I say unto you, Take no thought for your
life, what ye shall eat; neither for the body, what ye
shall put on.
<u>Verse 23</u>: The life is more than meat, and the body is
more than raiment.
<u>Verse 24:</u> Consider the ravens; for they neither sow
no reap; which neither have storehouse nor barn; and
God feedeth them: how much more are ye better than
the fowls?
<u>Verse 25</u>: And which of you with taking thought can
add to his stature one cubit?
<u>Verse 26:</u> If ye then be not able to do that thing which
is least, why take ye thought for the rest?
<u>Verse 27:</u> Consider the lilies how they grow, they toil
not, they spin not, and yet I say unto you, that
Solomon in all his glory was not arrayed like one of
these.
<u>Verse 28</u>: If then God so clothe the grass, which is

today in the field, and tomorrow is cast into the oven; how much more will he clothe you, O ye of little faith?

Verse 29: And seek not ye what ye shall eat, or what ye shall drink, neither be ye of doubtful mind.

Verse 30: For all these things do the nations of the world seek after: and your Father knoweth that ye have need of these things.

Verse 31: But rather seek ye the kingdom of God; and all these things shall be added unto you.

TREASURES IN HEAVEN-PROLONG THY DAYS ON EARTH

KEEP GOD'S COMMANDMENTS AND PROLONG THY DAYS UPON THE EARTH

Deuteronomy 4:40: Thou shalt keep therefore his statutes, and his commandments, which I command thee this day, that it may go well with thee, and with thy children after thee, and that thou mayest prolong thy days upon the earth, which the Lord thy God giveth thee, for ever.

Deuteronomy 5:16: Honour thy father and thy mother, as the Lord thy God hath commanded thee, that thy days may be prolonged, and that it may go well with thee, in the land which the Lord thy God giveth thee.

Deuteronomy 11:8-9

Verse 8: Therefore shall ye keep all the commandments which I command you this day, that ye may be strong, and go in and possess the land, whither ye go to possess it.

Verse 9: And that ye may prolong your days in the land, which the Lord sware unto your fathers to give unto them and to their seed, a land that floweth with milk and honey.

Matthew 6:19-24

Verse 19: Lay not up for yourselves treasures upon earth, where moth and rust doth corrupt, and where thieves break through and steal.

Verse 20: But lay up for yourselves treasures in heaven, where neither moth nor rust doth corrupt, and where thieves do not break through nor steal.

Verse 21: For where your treasure is, there will your heart be also.

Verse 22: The light of the body is the eye: if, therefore thine eye be single, thy whole body shall be full of light.

Verse 23: But if thine eye be evil, thy whole body shall be full of darkness. If therefore the light that is in thee be darkness, how great is that darkness!

Verse 24: No man can serve two masters: for either he will hate the one, and love the other; or else he will hold to the one, and despise the other. Ye cannot serve God and mammon.

SIX THINGS THE LORD HATES

Proverbs 6:16-19
A PROUD LOOK,

A LYING TONGUE,
HANDS THAT SHED INNOCENT BLOOD,

A HEART THAT DEVISETH WICKED
IMAGINATIONS,

FEET THAT BE SWIFT IN RUNNING TO MISCHIEF,

A FALSE WITNESS THAT SPEAKETH LIES,

AND HE THAT SOWETH DISCORD AMONG
BRETHREN

Proverbs 6:16-19
Verse 16:
These six things doth the Lord hate; yea, seven are an abomination unto him.
Verse 17:
A proud look, a lying tongue, and hands that shed innocent blood.
Verse 18:
An heart that deviseth wicked imaginations, feet that are swift in running to mischief.

<u>Verse 19:</u>
A false witness that speaketh lies, and he that soweth discord among brethren.

<u>Verse 20</u>
My son, keep thy father's commandment; and forsake not the law of thy mother.

<u>Verse 21:</u>
Bind them continually upon thine heart, and tie them about thy neck.

<u>Verse 22:</u>
When thou goest, it shall lead thee, when thou sleepest, it shall keep thee; and when thou awakest, it shall talk with thee.

<u>Verse 23:</u>
For the commandment is a lamp, and the law is light and reproofs of instruction are a way of life.

ANGELS:
THE BIBLE TALKS ABOUT ANGELS

Luke 12:8
Also I say unto you, Whosoever shall confess me before men, him shall the Son of man also confess before the angels of God.

Luke 15:10
Likewise, I say unto you, there is joy in the presence of the angels of God over one sinner that repenteth.

Luke 20:36
Neither can they die any more, for they are equal unto the angels; and are the children of God, being the children of the resurrection.

John 20:12
And seeth two angels in white sitting, the one at the head, and the other at the feet, where the body of Jesus had lain.

Revelation 3:5
He that overcometh, the same shall be clothed in white raiment; and I will not blot out his name out of the book of life, but I will confess his name before my Father, and before his angels.

I Timothy 3:16
And without controversy great is the mystery of
godliness; God was manifest in the flesh, justified in
the Spirit, seen of angels, preached unto the Gentiles,
believed on in the world, received up into glory.

Hebrews 13:2
Be not forgetful to entertain strangers; for thereby
some have entertained angels unawares.

Psalm 91:11
For he shall give his angels charge over thee, to
keep thee in all thy ways.

Matthew 13:49
So shall it be at the end of the world; the angels shall
come forth, and sever the wicked from among the
just.

Matthew 16:27
For the Son of man shall come in the glory of his
Father with his angels; and then he shall reward every
man according to his works.

Matthew 22:30
For in the resurrection they neither marry, nor are
given in marriage, but are as the angels of God in
heaven.

Matthew 24:36
But of that day and hour knoweth no man, no, not the
angels of heaven, but my Father only.

Luke 9:26

For whosoever shall be ashamed of me and of my words, of him shall the Son of man be ashamed, when he shall come in his own glory and in his Father's, and of the holy angels.

THE DEVIL: THE BIBLE TALKS ABOUT THE DEVIL

DEVIL, SERPENT, DRAGON, SATAN
(Biblical names for Satan)

I Corinthians 10:21:
Ye cannot drink the cup of the Lord, and the cup of devils; ye cannot be partakers of the Lord's table, and of the table of devils.

Revelation: 20:1-3
Verse 1: And I saw an angel come down from heaven, having the key of the bottomless pit and a great chain in his hand.
Verse 2: And he laid hold on the dragon, that old serpent, which is the Devil, and Satan, and bound him a thousand years.
Verse 3: And cast him into the bottomless pit, and shut him up, and set a seal upon him, that he should deceive the nations no more, till the thousand years should be fulfilled: and after that he must be loosed a little season.

Luke 8:12-13
Verse 12: Those by the way side are they that hear; then cometh the devil, and taketh away the word out of their hearts, lest they should believe and be saved.

<u>Verse 13</u>: They on the rock are they, which, when they hear, receive the word with joy; and these have no root, which for a while believe, and in time of temptation fall away.

<u>I John 3:8</u>:
He that committeth sin is of the devil; for the devil sinneth from the beginning. For this purpose the Son of God was manifested, that he might destroy the works of the devil.

<u>Revelation 12:9</u>:
And the great dragon was cast out, that old serpent, called the Devil, and Satan, which deceiveth the whole world: he was cast out into the earth, and his angels were cast out with him.

PSALM 100

Verse 1: Make a joyful noise unto the Lord, all ye lands.

Verse 2: Serve the Lord with gladness; come before his presence with singing.

Verse 3: Know ye that the Lord he is God; it is he that hath made us, and not we ourselves; we are his people, and the sheep of his pasture.

Verse 4: Enter into his gates with thanksgiving, and into his courts with praise: be thankful unto him, and bless his name.

Verse 5: For the Lord is good; his mercy is everlasting; and his truth endureth to all generations.

THE SHORTEST PSALM: PSALM 117

Verse 1: O praise the Lord, all ye nations: praise him, all ye people.

Verse 2: For his merciful kindness is great toward us: and the truth of the Lord endureth forever. Praise ye the Lord.

MUSICAL INSTRUMENTS
MENTIONED IN THE BIBLE

Revelation 18:21-22
Verse 21: And a mighty angel took up a stone like a great millstone, and cast it into the sea, saying, Thus with violence shall that great city Babylon be thrown down, and shall be found no more at all.
Verse 22: And the voice of harpers, and musicians, and of pipers, and trumpeters, shall be heard no more at all in thee; and no craftsman, of whatsoever craft he be, shall be found any more in thee; and the sound of a millstone shall be heard no more at all in thee.

I Corinthians 14:7-8:
Verse 7: And even things without life giving sound, whether pipe or harp, except they give a distinction in the sounds, how shall it be known what is piped or harped?
Verse 8: For if the trumpet give an uncertain sound, who shall prepare himself to the battle?
I Corinthians 15:52: In a moment, in the twinkling of an eye, at the last trump; for the trumpet shall sound, and the dead shall be raised incorruptible, and we shall be changed.

 Hebrews 12:19: And the sound of a trumpet, and the voice of words; which voice they that heard entreated that the word should not be spoken to them anymore.

<u>Matthew 24:31</u>: And he shall send his angels with a great sound of a trumpet, and they shall gather together his elect from the four winds, from one end of heaven to the other.

<u>Revelation 8:2</u>: And I saw the seven angels which stood before God; and to them were given seven trumpets.

<u>Revelation 8:6</u>: And the seven angels which had the seven trumpets prepared themselves to sound.

<u>Revelation 8:13</u>: And I beheld, and heard an angel flying through the midst of heaven, saying with a loud voice, Woe, woe, woe, to the inhabiters of the earth by reason of the other voices of the trumpet of the three angels, which are yet to sound!

<u>Revelation 9:14</u>: Saying to the sixth angel which had the trumpet, Loose the four angels which are bound in the great river Euphrates.

<u>Revelation 14:2</u>: And I heard a voice from heaven, as the voice of many waters, and as the voice of a great thunder; and I heard the voice of harpers harping with their harps.

<u>Revelation 15:1-2</u>

<u>Verse 1</u>: And I saw another sign in heaven, great and marvellous, seven angels having the seven last plagues; for in them is filled up the wrath of God.

<u>Verse 2</u>: And I saw as it were a sea of glass mingled with fire; and them that had gotten the victory over the beast, and over his image, and over his mark, and over the number of his name, stand on the sea of glass, having the harps of God.

TREES MENTIONED IN THE BIBLE

-A-

Algum Tree
2 Chronicles 2:8, 9:10, 9:11

Almond Tree
Ecclesiastes 12:5, Jeremiah 1:11

Apple Tree
Song of Solomon 2:13, Song of Solomon 8:5,
Joel 1:12

-B-

Bay Tree, Green
Psalm 37:35

Bird's Nest and Eggs
Deuteronomy 22:6-7

Box Tree
Isaiah 41:19, Isaiah 60:13

-C-

Cedar Tree
I Kings 4:33, Isaiah 41:19, Ezekiel 31:8,
Zechariah 11:2

Chestnut Tree
Ezekiel 31:8

-D-

Dry Tree, *General Reference*
Isaiah 56:3

-F-

Fig Tree
Judges 9:10-11, I Kings 4:25, I Kings 6:31-33, II
Kings 18:31, Psalm 27:18, Song of Solomon 2:13,
Isaiah 34:4, Isaiah 36:16, Jeremiah 8:13, Hosea 9:10,
Joel 1:7, Joel 1:12, Joel 2:22, Micah 4:4,
Habakkuk 3:17, Haggai 2:19, Zechariah 3:10,
Matthew 21:19-21, Matthew 24:32, Mark 11:13,
Mark 20-21, Mark 13:28, Luke 6:44, Luke 13:6-7,
Luke 21:29, John 1:48, John 1:50, Revelation 6:13

Fir Tree
I Kings 6:34, II Chronicles 3:5, Isaiah 41:19,
Isaiah 55:13, Isaiah 60:15, Ezekiel 31:8, Zechariah 11:2

Fruit Trees, General Reference
Genesis 1:11-12, Genesis 1:29, Genesis 3:3,
Leviticus 27:30

-G-

Green Tree, General Reference
Deuteronomy 12:2, I Kings 14:23, II Kings 16:4,
II Kings 17:10, Jeremiah 2:20, Jeremiah 3:6,
Jeremiah 3:13, II Chronicles 28:4, Isaiah 57:5,
Ezekiel 6:13, Ezekiel 17:24, Ezekiel 20:47, Luke 23:31

-J-
Juniper Tree
I Kings 19:4-5

-M-
Mulberry Tree
II Samuel 5:23
Myrtle Tree
Isaiah 41:19, Isaiah 55:13

-O-
Olive Tree
Deuteronomy 24:20, Judges 9:8-9, Psalm 52:8,
Isaiah 17:16, Isaiah 24:13, Jeremiah 11:16, Hosea 14:8,
Haggai 2:19, Romans 11:7, Romans 11:24, James 3:12

Oil Tree
Isaiah 41:19

Oak Tree
Isaiah 6:13, Ezekiel 6:13

-P-
Palm Tree
Judges 4:5, Psalm 92:12, Song of Solomon 7:78,
Exodus 15:27, Exodus 23:40, Jeremiah 10:5,
Ezekiel 41:18-19, Joel 1:12

Pine Tree
Isaiah 41:19, Isaiah 60:13

Pomegranate Tree
I Samuel 14:2, Joel 1:12, Haggai 2:19

Poplar Tree, Green
Genesis 30:37

-S-
Sycamine Tree
Luke 17:6

Sycamore Tree
Luke 19:14

Shittah Tree
Isaiah 41:19

-T-
Teil Tree
Isaiah 6:13

Tree of Life
Genesis 2:9, 3:24, Psalm 3:18, Psalm 11:30,
Psalm 13:12, Psalm 15:4, Revelation 2:7,
Revelation 22:2, Revelation 22:14
Numbers 6:4, Ezekiel 15:2, Ezekiel 15:6

-W-
Willow Tree
Ezekiel 17:5

SUMMARIES OF THE
BOOKS OF THE
OLD TESTAMENT

Genesis

The word "GENESIS" actually means the "beginning". Genesis is the first book of Moses.

Genesis documents the records of Adam and Eve and their beginning in the Garden of Eden.

Genesis is also a record of the lives of Noah, Abraham, Isaac, Jacob and Joseph from the beginning to approximately 1700 B. C. The book of Genesis tells us about life in general and the history.

We know from the book of Genesis that God created the entire universe, and it tells us that God's knowledge is true.

According to the book of Genesis, evil began because Adam and Eve did not obey God's instructions to them. They ate of the "tree of good and evil", which God had forbidden them to eat.

It is very interesting to follow the lineage of the first man and woman, their siblings, and their ages.

One of the most familiar stories of Genesis is that of Noah, who was instructed to build an ark. These instructions were given to Noah, because the people of the land had become exceedingly wicked and would not obey God's word.

Noah, his family, and two of every kind of animal and fowl were spared after 40 days and nights of rain.

NOTE: The Book of Genesis has 50 chapters

Exodus

In the book of Exodus, we learn of Moses' birth, how God taught him, and how he eventually led the Israelites out of their slavery.

Exodus brings to light the struggle of the Israelites, once being treated very well by Joseph, and then being put into slavery under a cruel king.

Exodus also tells us the story of Moses and his struggle with Pharaoh, King of Egypt, the Red Sea crossing, and his travel to Mount Sinai.

At Mt. Sinai, Moses gave the people the law (sometimes referred to as the "law of Moses"), and he instructed them in detail how to build the tabernacle.

God took care of the Israelites and eventually led them to be a "nation of God", not of man.

<u>NOTE</u>:   The Book of Exodus has 40 chapters

Leviticus

Leviticus is the third book of Moses. The meaning of the word Leviticus is "things about Levi". Jacob was blessed, and Levi was son number three.

Moses' descendants were appointed as priests; their mission was to take charge of the tabernacle and the religious activities of the country of Israel.

Leviticus is a religious manual to the priests. It contained religious direction, which the priests were admonished to enforce and observe for Israel.

Historically, it details the time (2 years) spent on Mt. Sinai.

The Book of Leviticus details how the priests should perform the religious observances daily. This was very important as to the direction of the Israelites in the future.

The information contained in Moses' third book gives

us, as Christians, direction for receiving God's blessings.

NOTE: The Book of Leviticus has 27 chapters.

Numbers

Numbers is the name derived from the counting of the Israelites on Mt. Sinai. Also, this refers to a second counting after the '40 years' travel through the wilderness.

The Book of Numbers depicts Moses' travels through the wilderness and tells about his journey as the Israelites came down from Mt. Sinai after being there approximately two years.

Faith and trust in God proved to be overwhelming, as the covenant people endured troubles and great difficulties.

The Israelites found favor with God, despite the fact that their faith and trust was not always as strong as it should have been.

NOTE: The Book of Numbers has 36 chapters.

Deuteronomy

Deuteronomy is the fifth book of Moses.

The Israelites camped just east of the River Jordan before crossing into the land of Canaan. Moses prepared the Israelites by providing a history of the things that transpired during the 40 years in the wilderness.

Moses stressed to this younger group of Israelites that God would always be faithful to them, while providing them also with the story of the older Israelites that had been so sinful against God in the past.

Moses strongly admonished them not to make the same mistakes of Israelites in the past, because God would not look favorably on them if they did not keep his laws.

Moses was 120 years old when he died in the land of Moab. He was buried in a valley in the land of Moab over against Beth-peor: but no man knows where his sepulchre is unto this day (Deuteronomy Chapter 34, Verse 6.)

NOTE: The Book of Deuteronomy has 34 chapters.

Joshua

In the book of Joshua, Joshua documents the Israelites crossing the River Jordan into the land of Canaan.

Joshua was the leader of the Israelite people and led them into a fierce battle against the kings who did not want them in their country.

Joshua was somewhat successful in bringing the tribes together in unification of the covenant of God.

Joshua won the battles against those who did not live in accordance with God's word. The Israelites, though successful in their battles in Canaan, faced many trials and tribulations. The Canaanites were hostile to them when they crossed the River Jordan, but finally the tribes came together.

Joshua was 110 years old when he died.

NOTE: The Book of Joshua has 24 chapters.

Judges

The Book of Judges describes life under King Saul, their leader, after the settlement in the land of Canaan.

There were many Israelite tribes, and Judges gives details of life as it existed there for several hundred years.

After crossing the River Jordan and settling in the land of Canaan, the Israelites were a Godly people and obeyed God's laws. However, eventually, the people became wicked and sinful again, and God was not happy with them. There were many foes sent by God as punishment for their wickedness. Finally, they repented once more.

There were 12 judges appointed to serve all the tribes.

Ironically, the lifestyle of the people was falling away from God, being punished, and coming back to God in the end.

This is the same lifestyle sadly that Christians today face. But, God is a loving God, and there is forgiveness for our sins through the crucifixion of our Lord, Jesus Christ.

Sadly enough, at that time, there was not an official king in Israel. The people did that which was right in their own eyes.

NOTE: The Book of Judges has 21 chapters

Ruth

The Book of Ruth tells the story of Ruth, the great grandmother of King David. Naomi was an Israelite woman, and one of her daughters-in-law was Ruth. Ruth's second marriage was to Boaz, who was quite wealthy.

The life and history during Ruth's time indicates that people considered 'foreigners' were accepted into the Israelite communities. This was preemptive of Gentiles being included into God's church. Ruth herself was a Gentile who was in the ancestry of our Lord Jesus Christ.

NOTE: The Book of Ruth has 4 chapters

I Samuel

The First Book of Samuel is also referred to as "The First Book of the Kings".

King David and King Saul are described in this book, which covers the period of 1050 B.C. To 960 B.C. King Saul and King David each reigned for a period of 40 years.

King Saul was a great protector of his people, but he did not obey God's commandments.

In Chapter 31, Verse 4, Saul committed suicide by falling on his own sword.

King David, during his 40-year reign, also was wicked and sinned against God. However, David saw the error of his ways, repented of his sins, and once again found favor with God.

NOTE: The Book of I Samuel has 31 chapters

II Samuel

The Second Book of Samuel is referred to as the "Second Book of the Kings".

King Saul was a great protector of his people, but he did not obey God's commandments as he should have.

David was the King of Judah. During his reign, David unified the people and asked God for forgiveness in his personal life of sin.

NOTE: The Book of II Samuel has 24 chapters

1 Kings

The First Book of the Kings is sometimes referred to as the Third Book of the Kings, describing reigns of all the kings of Israel.

The First Book of the Kings tells the stories of kings such as Solomon, Jeroboam, Asa, Jehoshaphat, Hezekiah, and Josiah.

Christians can learn from the stories of the kings in the first Book of Kings concerning the deterioration of morals, godliness, idolatry and the punishment that God provided.

NOTE: The Book of I Kings has 22 chapters

II Kings

The Second Book of the Kings is sometimes referred to as the Fourth Book of the Kings, describing reigns of the kings of Israel.

The Second Book of the Kings describes the alliance between Israel and Judah.

It also describes the details of Israel's fall and Israel's prosperous times.

The survival of Judah by Assyrian domination is also described.

The absorption of Judah by Babylonia is also described in this Second Book of Kings.

<u>NOTE:</u>   The Book of II Kings has 25 chapters

I & II Chronicles

The First and Second Books of Chronicles tell the stories of the kingdoms of King David and King Solomon.

The First Book of Chronicles concentrates on King David's dynasty.

The Second Book of Chronicles concentrates on King Solomon and his kingdom.

It also describes the history of the kings of Judah, the revolt of the ten tribes, the captivity of Babylonia, and the story of Cyrus allowing the Jews to go back to Jerusalem for the purpose of re-building the temple.

These books clearly show that the Lord was pleased, and He blessed the people who served him. It also demonstrates his punishment of the people who failed to keep his commandments.

These books reflect the desire of the Lord for christians to follow him and live a life of righteousness.

These books reflect the desire of the Lord for Christians to follow him, keep his commandments, and live a life of righteousness.

NOTE: The Book of I Chronicles has 29 chapters
        The Book of II Chronicles has 36 chapters

Ezra

The Book of Ezra tells us that Ezra was a scribe who secured a commission from the King of Persia to teach the Jews (who were still under Persian control) the law.

Ezra documented the stories of the people who returned from exile. He specifically documented the rebuilding of the temple.

Ezra was very concerned when he discovered that the Jews were marrying non-Jews as he felt they were not serving in the way of the Lord. He put an end to this practice and led them back to serving the Lord according to his Covenant.

Ezra's ministry to the people was to bring them back into the service of the Lord.

NOTE: The Book of Ezra has 10 chapters

Nehemiah

The Book of Nehemiah describes how Nehemiah felt when he heard the news that the Jews (who had returned from exile) were being abused by enemies in their community.

Nehemiah asked the King of Persia for permission to go to the Jewish community and set some parameters for those living there.

Nehemiah guided the Jews to build a wall around Jerusalem and encouraged families to live within those walls.

Nehemiah called a gathering of all the people, and asked Ezra to read the law to the people. After hearing Ezra read the law, the people agreed to obey the covenant. At that time, Nehemiah enforced the Sabbath rules.

We, as Christians, continue to be instructed and guided by the Holy Scriptures.

NOTE: The Book of Nehemiah has 13 chapters

Esther

The Book of Esther describes a beautiful young Jewish girl who captured the attention of the King of Persia.

Esther won a beauty contest, and she was then selected by the King of Persia to be his queen.

Esther loved her people and foiled a plot to destroy the Jewish people. Through Esther's loyalty to her people, the Jews were protected and the gospel was preserved.

NOTE: The Book of Esther has 10 chapters

Job

Job was a man that loved the Lord and served him faithfully. The Book of Job describes Job's trials and tribulations, a tragic story with a heartwarming ending.

He did not understand why bad things began to happen to him, as he had kept the Lord's commandments and served him faithfully.

Job lost all his fortune, his health became very poor, and all his children were dead.
Even though all these bad things happened to Job, he

kept his faith in the Lord. He knew that there had to be a good reason why this was happening to him, despite all the pain and suffering he went through during this time.

In the end, through Job's continued faith to the Lord, he was rewarded.

God gave Job twice the amount of wealth that he had before. Job had twice the number of sheep, oxen, she asses, and camels. God also now gave Job seven sons and three daughters.

God also blessed Job again as he lived another one hundred and forty years, four generations more.

NOTE: The Book of Job has 42 chapters

Psalms

The Book of Psalms contains poems and writings of different authors.

The Book of Psalms contains 150 of these beautiful poems, and a lot were written by David.

The spirit of these poems reflects a vast range of emotions that we Christians have today. The Book of Psalms details guilt, sin, prayers to the Lord for worship, praises to the Lord, and thankfulness for God's love.

The shortest psalm is Psalm 117, containing only two verses.

The longest psalm is Psalm 119, containing 176 verses.

NOTE: The Book of Psalms has 150 chapters

Proverbs

The Book of Proverbs is generally thought to be written by King Solomon.

The Book of Proverbs details wisdom, truth, loyalty to our God and is a good example of how we should conduct our daily lives.

Proverbs seems to tell us that we should live a God-oriented life, and that everything we do should be centered with God's will first.

Proverbs admonishes us to learn and study and truly become 'wise' in the ways of our Lord, Jesus Christ.

The spreading of the gospel to every nation is God's will for Christians today.

NOTE: The Book of Proverbs has 31 chapters

Ecclesiastes

It is unclear who wrote the Book of Ecclesiastes. It is possible that Solomon and other kings wrote this book filled with philosophy.

Possibly, it is a reflection of King Solomon and his life of wealth and privilege. Solomon did eventually discern that wealth was just 'vanity', and he began to contemplate what 'value' really meant in his life.

Solomon truly did finally realize through wisdom that he should fear God and that he should keep God's holy commandments.

Verse 14 of Chapter 12 sums it up this way: "For God shall bring every work into judgment, with every secret thing, whether it be good, or whether it be evil".

NOTE: The Book of Ecclesiastes has 12 chapters

Song of Solomon

The Book of Song of Solomon is a beautiful love story of King Solomon and a Shulamite girl.

They express their love for one another, and
it is a description of their marital feelings.

This book shows the connection between
marital love and God's love. God's love clearly shows
that he approves of the love between a married man
and his wife.

NOTE: The Book of Song of Solomon has 8 chapters.

Isaiah

Isaiah was one of the first 'writing' prophets.
Many of the others did not serve as 'writing'
prophets.

Isaiah's mission was to educate the people and tell
them that God was sovereign over any other
'false gods' that the people believed in.

Isaiah instructed the people that God's divine
deliverance was assured, and that the final
kingdom would eventually be established
through His Son, Jesus Christ.

NOTE: The Book of Isaiah has 66 chapters

SUMMARY OF THE OLD TESTAMENT

Jeremiah

Jeremiah, the Prophet, warned Jerusalem for many years that God would send the Babylonian army to punish them because their nation had become so ungodly.

This prophetic advice made Jeremiah very unpopular in Jerusalem, and he was hated by most of the people, including kings.

He was finally imprisoned as a traitor.

The fall of Jerusalem did occur, and Jeremiah escaped with some Jews and fled into the land of Egypt.

During the rest of Jeremiah's life, he continued to spread God's word to the people.

The Book of Jeremiah serves as a lesson to Christians today to spread God's word to everyone, no matter what trials and tribulations that occur as a consequence.

God is always with us in the spreading of his holy word.

NOTE: The Book of Jeremiah has 52 chapters

Lamentations

Biblical scholars generally think that the book of Lamentations was written by Jeremiah.

It tells the story about the Babylonian army destroying Jerusalem because the people had become so wicked, and they were not keeping the faith or the covenants of the Lord.

This book documents terrible disasters, but we still know and believe God's promise to protect his people.

NOTE: The Book of Lamentations has 4 chapters.

Ezekiel

During the Babylonian captivity, Ezekiel served as a prophet of God.

Ezekiel was constantly trying to get the Jews to repent of their sins, and promised them that God would eventually punish those that had captured them. Ezekiel told the people that God would restore

Jerusalem, and the holy temple would be re-built in Jerusalem.

The Jews were despondent in captivity, as they wanted to return to their land.

Finally, Israel was restored, and the Jews were allowed to return to their ancestral land.

NOTE: The Book of Ezekiel has 48 chapters

Daniel

The first half of the Book of Daniel describes the experiences of Daniel and his three friends, Hananiah, Mishael, and Azariah.

Daniel tells how the Lord blessed them, even through they were going through many trials and tribulations.

The last half of the Book of Daniel describes visions that were given to him by God.

NOTE: The Book of Daniel has 12 chapters.

Hosea

The Book of Hosea sternly warns against the idolatry being practiced by the people. The promise was that God would not abandon Israel, even though they would not keep his statutes and commandments.

The Book of Hosea serves Christians as a reminder that the churches should not forsake our Lord, Jesus Christ.

NOTE: The Book of Hosea has 14 chapters

Joel

The Book of Joel documents a terrible invasion of locusts, which eventually destroyed everything on the farmlands of Israel.

This locusts invasion was a punishment invoked upon the people because they would not repent of their sins and return to the ways of our Lord, Jesus Christ. This invasion also came with a warning of worse things to come if the people continued in their wicked ways.
Joel's prophecy was fulfilled, and the gospel was spread throughout all nations.

NOTE: The Book of Joel has 3 chapters

Amos

Amos was a common farmer who lived in the land of Judah.

Amos witnessed all around him the sins of idolatry, horrible treatment of the poor, greed, violence, and other evils.

Amos began to tell the people that God's judgment would come about through the land of Israel and Judah. He referenced God's judgment, such as fires, locust plagues, etc.

Amos made it a point to educate the people and let them know that Christians must adhere to God's commandments in their daily lives; they must keep his commandments and statutes.

The Book of Amos has 9 chapters

Obadiah

Obadiah had a message that God would pronounce his judgment against Edom.

Edom and Israel were enemy countries, and Obadiah told the Edomites that God would punish them because they were opposed to Israel, God's chosen country.

This is a good lesson to Christians today. God will make judgment on the enemies of Christ, and, according to the Lord's words, someday these enemies will be destroyed.

NOTE: The Book of Obadiah has only 1 chapter with 21 verses.

Jonah

The Assyrians were enemies of Israel. Jonah had been instructed to go and spread God's message in Nineveh, the capital city of the Assyrians.

Jonah carried the message of God to the Assyrians, they repented, and God did not cause devastation on Nineveh. This angered Jonah.

The message of this was to show that God's mercy was not just for his chosen people, the Israelites. Also in the Book of Jonah is the story of how Jonah was swallowed by a whale and regurgitated.

After Jesus died and rose again, his message was spread unto the Gentile nations also.

NOTE: The Book of Jonah has 4 chapters

Micah

Micah was also considered one of the 'writing' prophets and documented the events of his era.

Micah had strong condemnation for both Israel and Judah.

He prophesied that soon a ruler would come that would tell the people of God's peaceful reign.

This prophesy was fulfilled in the coming of the Lord, Jesus Christ.

NOTE: The Book of Micah has 7 chapters

Nahum

Nahum prophesied also to the people of Nineveh, and God's judgment was postponed because they repented of their sins.

Nineveh returned to their wickedness, and their destruction was inevitable. Nineveh was eventually destroyed by the Babylonians.

God's judgment of the wicked may only be postponed, because those who do not repent and keep God's commandments will be punished.

NOTE: The Book of Nahum has 3 chapters

Habakkuk

The Book of Habakkuk is written as if it were a conversation between the Prophet Habakkuk and God. The people of Judah were punished by the wicked Babylonians, and Habakkuk could not understand why God did this.

God replied to Prophet Habakkuk that eventually the Babylonians would also be punished for their wickedness. Habakkuk had a great sense of what was right and wrong, and his faith and trust in God continued. Sometimes our churches suffer at the hands of non-believers.

In reading our Bibles, we see God's wrath against those who will not repent of their sinful ways and keep his commandments.

But, then again, we see God's mercy and His forgiveness.

NOTE: The Book of Habakkuk has 3 chapters

Zephaniah

Zephaniah was a prophet during the reign of King Josiah, at a time when the Jews' wickedness still fiercely angered the Lord.

Zephaniah prophesied of impending doom, and the God-fearing King Josiah decided to purge the idolaters from Judah.

But, in the end, God's wrath did descend on Judah and the surrounding nations.

We look forward to the final day when God will judge all evil and reward the Christians, the poor and the needy.

NOTE: The Book of Zephaniah has 3 chapters.

Haggai

The Jews who returned to Jerusalem after the Babylonian captivity period was ministered to by the prophet Haggai.

He asked the exiled Jews who returned to Jerusalem to make the temple re-building their first priority.

This temple re-building did run into some problems, as there were neighbors who were not in agreement with this project.

This is a good lesson for Christians today who

are trying to build and grow our churches.
There will always be obstacles, but perseverance
is the key.

NOTE: The Book of Haggai has 2 chapters

Zechariah

The rebuilding of the temple had been delayed
because of opposition. So Zechariah was joined by
Haggai in trying to persuade the Jews to rebuild the
temple.

Finally, the temple was built, and Zechariah had a
long range vision of the entire kingdom being
restored.

Although we have not seen the re-establishment of
the Jewish kingdom happen yet physically, we know
that Christ, our Savior, will return one day to this
earth.

NOTE: The Book of Zechariah has 14 chapters

Malachi

Malachi was the last of the 'writing' prophets. He also
lived around the time of Nehemiah and Ezra.

He strongly warned the exiles who had returned that their sinfulness would be punished.

Malachi spoke not only of the past, but of a messenger that was to prepare for the coming of the Lord to the temple.
This messenger was John the Baptist, who baptized Jesus.

We learn about God's mercy and grace and look forward to God's future plans for us.

NOTE: The Book of Malachi has 4 chapters.

SUMMARIES OF THE
BOOKS OF THE
NEW TESTAMENT

Matthew

The Jewish people had learned of a coming Messiah, and it was Matthew that convinced them that Jesus would come. Matthew, through genealogy, traced Jesus' lineage back to Abraham.

Matthew often told of the miracles, and he told them that Christ would not at this time set up an earthly kingdom, despite what the Jews believed.

Matthew also provided guidance that Jesus' ministry was for all the nations, rather than just for the Jews.

Matthew (sometimes referred to as Levi) was one of the 12 disciples; therefore, he had true experiences with Jesus.

NOTE: The Book of Matthew has 28 chapters

Mark

The gospel of Mark distinctly refers to the Roman people. John Mark, however, was not one of the 12 disciples; he was referred to by Peter as 'Marcus my son'.

It is thought that a lot of Mark's writings perhaps came from information obtained from Peter.

The Romans could not understand why Christians would follow the teachings of someone who was crucified as a common criminal.

In the end, God proved the opposition (the Romans) wrong by raising Jesus from the dead. Mark emphasized that Jesus was correct in his teachings, statutes and commandments, and that he truly was the Son of God.

NOTE: The Book of Mark has 16 chapters.

Luke

It is generally believed that Luke's style of writing was the best of all the gospels.

Luke traveled a great deal of the time with the Apostle Paul. Luke's main mission was to convince the people that Jesus really was the Son of God, and his teachings were to be believed.

Luke described and detailed Jesus' ministry, which included not only men, but women also.

He stressed Jesus' love and concern for the poor people, the infirmed, and those of less fortunate circumstances.

Luke explained to the people that Jesus' ministry was not only for the Jews, but also the Gentiles.

The Book of Luke is the only book to directly reflect Jesus' ascension into heaven.

Chapter 24, Verses 50 and 51 tell of Jesus' ascension into heaven.

NOTE: The Book of Luke has 24 chapters

John

The Book of John was written by the Apostle John, the disciple that Jesus dearly loved.

The book of John is written describing the 7 signs that Jesus gave to let the people know he was the true Messiah.

He turned water into wine, healed the sick,
performed other miracles, and raised Lazarus from
the dead.

Many people of that period had trouble believing that
Jesus was the Messiah. Those who did believe in Jesus
were very loyal and passionate in their faith.

NOTE: The Book of John has 21 chapters

Acts

The Book of Acts was also written by Luke.

Acts is a continuation of the gospel of Luke
with the ascension of Jesus into heaven.

The gospel was spread from Nazareth to
Jerusalem to the Roman empire.

Luke was quite descriptive about the ministry of
Peter, Philip, Stephen, Saul, and the persecutions
of those preaching the gospel.

Many of the writings of Luke were gathered
as he accompanied Paul on missionary
trips.

NOTE: The Book of Acts has 28 chapters

Romans

Paul wrote the Book of Romans while still in Corinth. In this book, Paul's writings explain the things he would have told the Romans, if he had been there.

He explained God's promises in the Old Testament and assured them that the coming of Christ was the fulfilling of God's word.

From the time of Adam's sin, everyone was now in the evils of the world. They were subjected to God's wrath because of their wickedness.

The Israelites still remained a sinful nation, despite the warnings that God's wrath would be shown to them.

God declared those who believed in his son to be a righteous people, provided that they would continue to believe and serve Christ in the Holy Spirit.

NOTE: The Book of Romans has 16 chapters

I Corinthians

The Book of I Corinthians describes the trouble in the church at Corinth. Paul was distressed to learn of these troubles, and he described each one. Paul offered his advice to the church concerning these divisions.

Paul felt that Corinth was a very immoral city, and this immorality certainly contributed to the problems at the church. He advised them to expel any church member who was unrepentant for incest, to avoid sexual morality, to refrain from lawsuits, not to eat food sacrificed to idols, to dress appropriately for public worship, and many other matters that were deemed immoral.

He also advised Christians to convince the people who were denying the resurrection; and to assure them that Christ was actually resurrected according to God's will.

NOTE: The Book of I Corinthians has 16 chapters

II Corinthians

Many of the people in Corinth did not agree with Paul's previous letter (I Corinthians).

Paul had to deal with the denial of his apostolic authority, and therefore, his reputation with the people was poor.

Paul assured the Corinthians that his ministry was from God. Paul described his many sufferings because of his gospel ministry.

Paul was there to preach God's word and not to tear down the Church at Corinth. Paul wanted them to grow in the Spirit of the gospel and to grow in faith, dedication, obedience and love.

NOTE: The Book of II Corinthians has 13 chapters

Galatians

Galatians was believed to be written to the churches in Southern Galatia. These churches were started by Barnabas and Paul on their first missionary trip to the area.

There was a great influence by Judaizers who were teaching that Gentile Christians had to observe Jewish laws while also believing in Christ.

Their influence was beginning to take effect on the Galatians and directly challenged Paul's teachings. They Insisted that Paul was not one of the twelve apostles, and he was only telling part of the truth about eternal salvation.

Paul insisted that righteousness and Christianity did not come by observing Jewish law; it came from faith in the Lord, Jesus Christ.

Paul advised the people not to believe this theory and

to stay steadfast in their Christian beliefs.

NOTE: The Book of Galatians has 6 chapters.

Ephesians

Some scholars believe that the Epistle of Apostle Paul was a letter for all the churches around Ephesus.

Paul wrote from prison describing the conflict b between Jews and Gentile Christians. The tension between the Jewish people and the Gentile Christians was affecting the church and could split Christians into two separate groups. Paul feared this would eventually affect the dedication of the people of the church.

Paul taught the people that it was God's will that the gospel also be preached to the Gentiles   In Chapter 3, Verses 8 and 9, Paul speaks of preaching among the Gentiles.

Paul believed that bringing the Jewish people and the Gentiles together would bring stronger unity to the church.

NOTE: The Book of Ephesians has 6 chapters

Philippians

The Epistle of Paul the Apostle to the Philippians is thought to be a 'thank-you letter' that was written by Paul while he was in prison.

This letter was sent to the church in Philippi because they had sent him gifts while he was in prison. They generally supported Paul while he was awaiting trial.

Paul was quite detailed in telling the Christians about his personal goals and his future plans, and he urged them to always follow the example of Christ. Paul expressed his appreciation for their support.

NOTE: The Book of Philippians has 4 chapters

Colossians

Paul had to send all his writings from prison by personal messenger. Paul used a messenger by the name of Tychicus to deliver the letters to the Ephesians, Colossians and to Philemon. One interesting fact was that when he sent Tychicus to deliver these letters, he also asked him to take a runaway slave back to his Colossae master.

While in prison, Paul told the churches of the false philosophy called Gnosticism.

Gnosticism is a belief that the body is evil, but the spirit is good, that the body is actually a prison where the soul resides. Therefore, they believed that Christ could not have had a human body, because the body was evil.

Paul taught that God actually was within the body of Jesus, and Jesus' death brings us closer to God.

Paul's simple message was that all Christians should not have sins of the flesh, but rather have faith and entertain the Holy Spirit within us for adherence to the will of God.

NOTE: The Book of Colossians has 4 chapters

I Thessalonians

The Book of I Thessalonians is generally thought to be the first existing letter that Paul wrote.

Paul left Thessalonica abruptly and was joined by Timothy a short time later.

The Thessalonians did not understand what advantage it was to them to be a Christian if someone died before Christ returned to the earth and established his kingdom. They felt that those who died would not be able to receive the blessings Christ had promised upon his return. Paul explained to them that Christ was the Messiah, and that he would raise them from the dead (just as he was raised from the dead in the resurrection). Paul testified that those who are alive when Christ returns will be equal to those who have passed before them. They will all ascend into heaven together, just as Christ ascended into heaven. Paul's message was that all Christians should be prepared, for no man knows the hour that our Savior will return to earth.

NOTE: The Book of I Thessalonians has 5 chapters

II Thessalonians

Paul wrote the II Book of Thessalonians shortly after the first Book of Thessalonians.

Paul wrote this book because of the problems the Thessalonian people still had in believing the return of Christ to the earth.

Paul wrote that the second coming of Christ had not yet occurred, as this was an erroneous belief among the people.

Paul told them that 'certain things' must be fulfilled before the Lord returns. He told them that many refused to believe the truth, a falling away from the Church would occur, and that a 'man of sin' would be revealed, among other signs.

NOTE: The II Book of Thessalonians has 3 chapters.

I Timothy

The First Epistle of Paul the Apostle to Timothy describes Timothy, who had journeyed with Paul in his evangelistic work for many years.

Timothy was pastor in charge of the church in Ephesus while Paul traveled to Macedonia.

Timothy's mission was to rectify the false teachings and erroneous doctrines being taught by the men of Ephesus. He was also directed to make sure that public prayers were conducted in the proper way.

Paul gave Timothy instructions on how to care for the widows and most importantly how Timothy should conduct himself.

Timothy also had a mission to discourage the Gnosticism theory that was affecting the churches.

NOTE: The Book of I Timothy has 6 chapters.

II Timothy

In the Book of II Timothy, Christians in Rome were being persecuted under the reign of Emperor Nero.

Due to the persecution, Paul was arrested once again. His friend Luke remained with him all during his trial, which was not going in Paul's favor.

Paul wrote a letter to Timothy and asked Timothy to bring Mark with him to Rome.

It is thought that II Timothy was Paul's last existing letter. It stressed to Timothy to carry on his (Paul's) work. Timothy was asked to follow Paul's example and, despite persecutions, to carry on the word of Jesus Christ.

Timothy was admonished to preach against the false teachers and to spread the words of Jesus Christ, the Messiah.

NOTE: The II Book of Timothy has 4 chapters

Titus

Paul left Titus in Crete to continue preaching the gospel, to appoint elders in the churches. Paul gave

Titus specific guidelines and instructions for his preaching there. He also asked Titus to make sure he told the people that they were to obey the law there and live peaceably with all men.

Once Titus had finished this work, he joined Paul in Nicopolis.

NOTE: The Book of Titus has 3 chapters

Philemon

The Book of Philemon tells the story of a slave named Onesimus, who had run away from his master. Somehow, Onesimus found his way to Paul in Rome. At this time, Onesimus was converted to Christianity.

Paul convinced Onesimus that in good faith, he should return to his master, Philemon.

Paul actually wrote Philemon a letter asking him to receive Onesimus back into his service, treat him kindly and receive him as a brother in Christ.

Paul's friend Tychicus took Onesimus back to Philemon and gave Philemon Paul's letter.

NOTE: The Book of Philemon has 25 verses.

Hebrews

There are a lot of 'unknowns' about the Book of Hebrews.

It was written by an 'unknown' author, at an 'unknown' place, and at an 'unknown' date.

Hebrews details that Jesus is superior to anyone else, and especially over Judaism. It also states that the new covenant is superior to the old covenant.

This book reiterates that Christians should never stray away from Jesus, and they should always believe in the living God. They should never stop believing in Christ, for there is a promise that Christ's kingdom will be established upon his second coming to earth.

NOTE: The Book of Hebrews has 13 chapters

James

In the Bible, there were actually two men named 'James' among the twelve apostles.

The one that is thought to be the author of this book is 'James', the brother of Jesus. He became a believer after Jesus ascended to heaven.
James was very troubled that people who called themselves Christians were not living a righteous life,

according to the statutes and commandments of
Jesus. Once they were converted, they continued
living a sinful life. James advised them that faith
without a good Christian lifestyle was dead.

James preached to the people about good examples of
Christian life, patience even during suffering, treating
the rich and the poor the same, being careful about
the words that come out of their mouths, and keeping
their faith during trials and tribulations.

NOTE: The Book of James has 5 chapters

I Peter

The apostle Peter wrote this book because he knew
the people were suffering a lot of trials and
tribulations in this area of the country (now known
as Turkey). In this letter, he asked them to keep their
faith through these terrible times.

He stressed there is salvation in the resurrection of
Jesus, a sign of God's power.

God expects us to keep our faith no matter the trials
and tribulations we endure. This includes living and
obeying the law as well as living peaceably with all
men.

NOTE: The Book of I Peter has 5 chapters

II Peter

Peter's number one concern in this letter was to remain steadfast in warning the people about false teachers.

There were many, many Gnostic (false) teachers, who seemed to be gaining the edge with the people.

Peter pointed out how God's wrath punished the people in the Old Testament because they went about their sinful ways and against the teachings of Christ.

Peter was adamant in pointing out to the people that in the future, God would again send his wrath down and destroy sinful and wicked men.

He stated God would establish 'new heavens' and a 'new earth'. These new heavens and the new earth would be inhabited by the righteous people.

NOTE: The Book of II Peter has 3 chapters

I John

The First Epistle of John was probably written in John's later years. It is a letter of general nature with specific warning of false Gnostic teachings, which seemed to be gaining credibility in the communities.

John testified to the people that Jesus did indeed have

a real body, as he had been with Jesus, seen and heard him, spoken to him, and touched him.

John pointed out that all Christians have sinned, that they have mortal bodies, that they must repent and be forgiven of their sins and receive salvation.

Also, John points out that all Christians should model their lives by the example of Jesus' life.

NOTE: The Book of I John has 5 chapters

II John

When John refers to the 'elect lady and her children' (Verse 1), he is probably referring to the church and the people within, rather than a real 'family'.

John was sending a warning to the church about false teachers who wanted the people to believe in the Gnostic philosophy.
He once again reiterated that Jesus did have a real body, and the Christians should not accept these false teachings.

NOTE: The Book of II John has 13 verses

III John

The Third Epistle of John talks about lay preachers and how some of the very influential people in the Churches rejected them.

So, at this time, John felt it necessary to write a letter to Gaius, who was a very important person in the church.

John asked Gaius, to show these lay preachers his hospitality and respect, which many other church elders had refused to do.

NOTE: The Book of III John has only 14 verses

Jude

Jude was thought to be another brother of our Lord, Jesus Christ.

Jude also made a great effort to educate the people about the false teaching of Gnosticism.

Jude also speaks about two 'non-biblical' books and how Christians should stay strong in their true faith and belief in the Lord, Jesus Christ.

NOTE: The Book of Jude has only 25 verses

Revelation

The Book of Revelation describes a series of powerful visions that God gave to John about Christ. The general theme in these visions was about the continuing work of Christ from heaven, basically by spreading the gospel throughout all nations.

John talks about the vision and how Christ analyzed each of the seven churches in Asia.

In one of John's visions, he saw the throne of God, and Jesus was pictured as a lamb. He saw, in this vision, the opening of the 7 seals of a scroll, 7 angels emptying 7 bowls of God's wrath, 7 angels blowing trumpets, God's holy city coming down from heaven, and the destruction of all evil.

The Book of Revelation is basically symbolic, to remind all Christians that Christ is indeed still doing his work today from heaven.

Revelation explains God's wrath against a sinful world. It explains the promise of an ultimate victory by Christ, bringing all earthly struggles to an end.

NOTE: The Book of Revelation has 22 chapters

ARTWORK

AND

WRITINGS

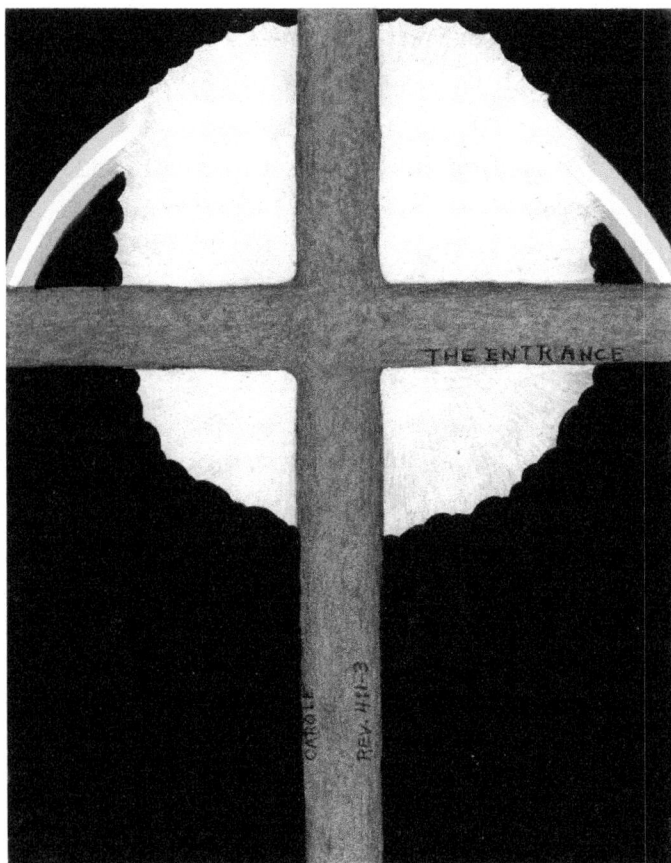

THE ENTRANCE

CAROL P

REV. 4:1-3

JACOB'S LADDER

COLORS OF THE EPHOD

I AM WHAT I AM

I Corinthians 15:10:
But by the grace of God, I am what I am: and his
grace which was bestowed upon me was not in vain;
but I labored more abundantly than they all: yet not
I, but the grace of God which was with me.

So, I am what I am by the Grace of God,

*I know I am terribly imperfect,
*But Christ refuses to abandon me or to give up
on me,
*He bestows upon me unexpected blessings and His
love,
*He is very patient with me when I don't get through
life's trials and tribulations too well,
*He listens to every prayer that I send to him, answers
them for my needs, and shows me that some prayers
just do not need to be answered!
*God comforts me through the Spirit of His Love,
when I don't think I can make it through another
minute, hour, or day,
*He gives me strength through my family, and that
helps hold everything together,

*He sends me beautiful friends to show me that life is fun and worthwhile, and that I should not take myself too seriously!

*He sends me knowledge to show me that others may be worse off than I am,

*He makes me realize that I need to be compassionate and more supportive with others, realizing that they may be facing a bigger battle than they care to reveal.

*He instills in me a desire to help someone, even if only in some small way, EVERYDAY.

*He asks of me, only that I keep his commandments, repent of my sins, love Him, spread His word, and make a conscientious effort to make Christian decisions for myself and others, and to LIVE by HIS WORDS.

I ALWAYS ASK WHAT WOULD JESUS DO?
IT IS STILL A BEAUTIFUL WORLD THAT OUR GOD GAVE US!!

MY PRAYER TODAY, LORD

Dear Lord:

*Please give me the strength that I need to be a better person,
*Help me to see the frivolity of my own personal needs when a friend is in crisis,
*Help me to be a shining light when that friend needs help,
*Help me to be eager to help with a willing heart when asked,
*Help me to show someone every day that I care about them,
*Help me to send someone a card of caring thoughts in their darkest hours,
*Help me to show loving kindness to someone I don't know,
*Help me to offer them words of encouragement,
*Help me to spread your word and let my life be an example of Christian love,
*Help me to hold in my anger when someone says something I don't like,
*Help me to offer words of kindness and assistance for the poor,
*Help me to use my latter days in a way that will be pleasing to thee,
*For it is only you Lord that we have to please on earth, not our fellow man,

*Help me always to lend a hand to help others,
with a very willing heart,
*Help me to encourage others to study and
keep your commandments,
*Help me to inspire others to receive you
as their Lord,
*Help me to teach the children through MY
words and deeds to be soldiers for you,
*Help me encourage others to 'Seek first your
Kingdom' and make you FIRST in their life,
*Help me, Lord, to not just 'say the words',
but to lead by example,
*Help me to stay positive, stay on the solid ground
and not waiver in my faith,
*Help me to forgive others when I hear that
someone has said unkind words about me,
*Help me to turn that around and make it
a positive, rather than a negative,
*Help me to learn more forgiveness, for as you
said, "Father, forgive them, for they know
not what they do",
*When I cross that River Jordan, Lord, I want
you to say, "Welcome my child, job well
done on earth".

Author: Carole Williams © 2016

CHILDREN

LOVE OF A CHILD-A LITTLE GIRL

*When our child is born, we only ask that she is healthy,

*Wow! She is finally here with pretty pink skin, ten little fingers and ten little toes,

*Gosh, she looks just like me,

*Well, honey, she does have your features, too,

*We now have a FAMILY – You, me, and our little one,

*Aren't we blessed by God with this precious little angel,

*Our baby is so little and so beautiful,

*This little angel gift you gave us is so precious to us, and we are thankful to you,

*Our baby is defenseless, helpless, looking up to us to smother her with our love,

*To help her grow and keep her safe, every minute, every hour, every day, every month, every year,

*We are thankful for God's blessing and promise to raise her in a Christian home,

*There will be many prayers, many tears, many moments of joy brought to our family by our little one.

*There will be moments when there are problems we can't solve,

*But, Lord, you said if we'd ask we would receive it,

and you would always be there to hear our prayers
*And if we keep your commandments, our days
   would be prolonged on this earth,
*So, Lord, here we are on bended knees,
*Asking for the help that we know only comes from
you.
 *We saw her first smile today, look how cute she is,
*Quick, get the camera honey, I don't want to miss
another smile,
*She sure is growing, just can't wait until she takes
her
   first steps,
*Ten months now, and she's walking!
*Wow, she took ten steps today, just look at her go,
*How the time passes, she's in those terrible two's
now,
*We will correct her with gentleness, patience and
love,
*We shall teach her right from wrong and about her
   Lord, Jesus Christ,
*We will TAKE her to Church and STAY THERE with
her,
*We will have daily prayers and meal blessings,
*Can you believe it honey, she's starting her first day
at school,
*Where do the years go; only yesterday God blessed
us with her beautiful presence,
*The years fly by, she is a TEENAGER now,
*We hope through her Christian home values that she
will   grow up to be a responsible adult,

*She loves to help others; especially those with special
   needs,
*She is a good student; she is a community volunteer,
*We are so proud of her and beam with pride every
day,
*Can you believe it honey, she's graduated high
school, and this is her first day of college,
*The years fly by, and she has graduated now from
college,
*Our years are quickly passing by; we now have
grandchildren,
*Those grandchildren are the apples of our eyes,
*Would you like to see pictures of my grandchildren?
*Isn't this what every grandparent says,
*The years fly by, Lord, and you have taken care of
us,
*You have blessed us with material blessings and our
   beautiful grandchildren,
*Now, they are taking care of us in our later years,
*And our life has come FULL CIRCLE,
*Through your Amazing Grace, Heavenly Father,
*To whom we give all the praise, honor and Glory,
*Until we reach our Heavenly Mansion,
*Forever and Ever, Amen.

Author: Carole Williams
© 2016

CHILDREN

LOVE OF A CHILD-A LITTLE BOY

*Wow! Pretty pink skin, ten little fingers and ten
    little toes,
*Gosh, he looks just like me,
*Well, honey, he does have your features, too,
*We now have a FAMILY – You, me, and our little
one,
*Aren't we blessed by God with this precious little
angel,
*Our little guy is so little and handsome,
*Lord, we submit daily prayers, that's all we ask of
you,
*This little angel gift is so precious to us and we are
    thankful to you,
*Our baby is defenseless, helpless, looking up to us to
smother him with our love,
*To help him grow and keep him safe,
*Every minute, every hour, every day, every month,
    every year,
*We share in God's blessing and promise to
    raise him in a Christian home,
*There will be many prayers, many tears, many
    moments of joy brought to our family by our
    little fellow,
*Through this tiny, tiny little bundle of joy,
*There will be moments when there are problems we

can't solve,
*But, you said if we'd ask we would receive it, and
that you would always receive our prayers,
*And if we keep your commandments, our days
would be prolonged on this earth,
*So, Lord, here we are on bended knees,
*Asking for the help that we know only
comes from you.
 *We saw his first smile today, look how cute he is,
*Quick, get the camera, honey, I don't want to miss
another smile,
*He sure is growing, just can't wait until he takes his
first steps,
*Eleven months now, and he's running all over the
place,
*How the time passes, he's in those terrible two's
now,
*We will correct him with gentleness and love,
*We shall teach him right from wrong and about his
Lord, Jesus Christ,
*We will TAKE him to Church and STAY THERE
with him,
*We will have daily prayers and meal blessings,
*Can you believe it, he's starting his first day at
school,
*Where do the years go; only yesterday he blessed us
with his beautiful presence,
*The years fly by, he is a TEENAGER now,
*We hope through his Christian home values that he
will grow up to be a responsible adult,
*He loves to help others; especially those who have

special needs,
*He is a good student; he is a community volunteer,
*We are so proud of him and beam with pride,
*Can you believe it honey, he's graduated high school, and this is his first day of college,
*The years fly by, and he has graduated now from college,
*Our years are quickly passing by; we now have grandchildren,
*Those grandchildren are the apples of our eyes,
*Would you like to see pictures of my grandchildren?
*Isn't this what every grandparent says,
*The years fly by, Lord, and you have taken care of us,
*You have blessed us with many material blessings and our grandchildren,
*Now, they are taking care of us in our later years,
*And our life has come FULL CIRCLE,
*Through our Heavenly Father's Grace, to whom we give all the praise and Glory,
*Until we reach our Heavenly Mansion,
*Forever and Ever, Amen.

Author: Carole Williams
© 2016

OUR LOVED ONES -
OH HOW WE LOVE THEM!

Who are our 'loved ones'?

We all cherish our loved ones; whether they are a child, a Mother, Father, sister, brother, uncle, aunt, grandmother, grandfather, or even cherished friends, mentors, neighbors, or our church family.

How our heart hurts when we lose one.

But we, as believers, know that once they leave this earth, it is not the end as referenced in this verse:

Matthew 12:32: And whosoever speaketh a word against the Son of man, it shall be forgiven him: but whosoever speaketh against the Holy Ghost, it shall not be forgiven him, *neither in this world, neither in the world to come.*

Titus 2:12: Teaching us that, denying ungodliness and worldly lusts, we should live soberly, righteously, and godly, in this **_present world._**

Heaven-Heavenly Mansions
John 14:2-3
Verse 2: In my Father's house are many
Mansions: if it were not so, I would have told
you. I go to prepare a place for you.
Verse 3: And if I go and prepare a place for you,
I will come again, and receive you unto myself;
that where I am, there ye may be also.

Revelation 21:4: And God shall wipe away
all tears from their eyes, and there shall be
no more death, neither sorrow, nor crying,
neither shall there be any more pain, for the
former things are passed away.

We must NEVER, EVER let the memories
of our loved ones fade, because we must
preserve them for our children and
grandchildren. Those memories are so precious
and bring us happiness during the periods when
we are feeling low.

We shall see our loved ones once again, in
Heaven, and what a joyful reunion that
will be, according to the wonderful promise
of our Lord, Jesus Christ.

Author: Carole Williams © 2016

OUR WORDS

There were words of wisdom that I heard many
long years ago, but I can't even remember
who spoke them. These words made a lot of
sense to me and have always remained with me . . .

Always be careful of the words you speak
because these words go. . . . . .

"From your lips to our Heavenly Father's ears"

God is our Heavenly Father, and he knows our
EVERY THOUGHT, before we even put that
thought into words.

Whether we realize it or not, our words to others
can make a difference in their lives.

We have two choices for the words that come
out of our mouths . . .

We can speak POSITIVE Christian words that
uplift and inspire others, or

We can speak NEGATIVE, hurtful words that tear
people down and cause negative emotional
scars.

When you get angry with others, get into the
habit of saying silently to yourself, "ZIP MY LIPS",
"ZIP MY LIPS". God doesn't want us to respond in
anger, even though some people are ugly to us.

*You will be surprised at the number of times you will
begin to feel that making your point or being right is
NOT IMPORTANT AT ALL!*

WHAT WILL YOUR WORDS SAY TODAY?

Will your words show your humbleness or
your anger,

Will your words show you to be a thoughtful
person, helping others along life's way,

Will your words comfort someone today,

Or, will your words hurt someone and add pain
to their day,

Will your words inspire a child today,

And help them become a positive child,

Or will your words tear down their
self-confidence and make them angry,
Will your words show someone you are their
friend and that you genuinely want to be supportive

of them,
Will your words inspire someone today to be a
better person,

Will your words reflect the message of Jesus
and show them you are not ashamed of
your Lord.

Will your words show you to be a SHINING
STAR to others, just as Jesus was,

WORDS ARE GIFTS FROM GOD, so please
don't think that you do not have any gifts
or talents,

You can call someone today, just to let them know
you are thinking about them. Let them know you care
and that they are important to you.

Author: Carole Williams
© 2016

Made in the USA
Las Vegas, NV
04 January 2022